GET PLUCKY
WITH THE
UKULELE

An Hachette UK Company
www.hachette.co.uk

First published in Great Britain in 2014 by Cassell,
an imprint of Octopus Publishing Group Limited,
Endeavour House, 189 Shaftesbury Avenue,
London WC2H 8JY

www.octopusbooks.co.uk
www.octopusbooksusa.com

Distributed in the US by Hachette Book Group USA,
1290 Avenue of the Americas, 4th and 5th Floors, New York,
NY 10020, USA

Distributed in Canada by Canadian Manda Group,
664 Annette St, Toronto, Ontario, Canada M6S 2C8

ISBN: 978-1-84403-790-2

Printed and bound in China.

Commissioning Editor Hannah Knowles
Art Director Jonathan Christie
Designer Jaz Bahra
Senior Editor Leanne Bryan
Photographer Brent Darby
Illustrator Jonny Hannah
Copy Editor Holly Kyte
Proofreader Emma Clegg
Indexer Isobel McLean
Assistant Production Manager
  Lucy Carter

GET PLUCKY

WITH THE

UKULELE

A QUICK AND EASY GUIDE

TO ALL THINGS UKE

◎◎◎◎◎◎◎◎◎◎◎◎◎◎◎◎◎◎◎◎◎

BY WILL GROVE-WHITE

CONTENTS

FOREWORD

BY WILL'S OLD FRIEND, COLLEAGUE AND (JUST POSSIBLY) MENTOR, GEORGE HINCHLIFFE

Dear reader, you have in your hands the philosopher's stone of the ukulele world. It is my favourite of all ukulele books.

Music should be fun. Music should be playful. Music is play, even if it's your work. And books should be challenging, stimulating and lively. This book is all those things. What's the point of a book about an instrument if it doesn't make you want to play it, or doesn't deepen your understanding of, and interest in the whole thing? Given that I've played the uke since 1960, you might think I would be jaded by now. Not any more. I'm cured! This book has made me interested in the ukulele again.

Along with Kitty Lux, Andy Astle and Jo Brindley, I founded the Ukulele Orchestra of Great Britain in London in the 1980s - our first public appearance was in 1985. We started The Strelzi Club at a now-defunct Islington pub called The Empress of Russia. We used to get 'Gig of the Week' notices in *Time Out* magazine and *City Limits* - probably because punters found it all fun, unpredictable and anarchic, but also because, back then, it was rare to find players of the wooden ukulele (or the 'bonzai guitar' as we christened it), as opposed to the banjo-ukulele. Any other players we came across tended to perform solo or use the uke as a novelty instrument in a conventional band.

We had only ukuleles in the orchestra, a purist tendency which in those days was regarded as distinctly odd. Now, however, with similar 'orchestras' of ukuleles firmly established as the norm in many countries, it is hard to conceive of the world before the current ukulele boom.

When he was 14 years old, Will Grove-White read about our club in the *Mail on Sunday*. Finding that our wacky/individualist/anarchic concept and our twanging sound chimed with his own tastes, he became a fan - one of the 'early adopters'. He came along to our performances on Friday nights, experiencing our 'depraved musicology' and also that of our guest artists. It was a strange mix of boozers, jaded rockers, journalists, glamorous fashion types, artists and crazies at the club. You should have seen the audience, too!

I sometimes worried about the damage all this might do to Will's psyche at such an impressionable age, and what he might end up doing with his life. He was a pretty good ukulele player even then, though. Between us - he, the youthful prodigy, and me, the old hand - we probably had a shared level of musical maturity. It was fun to play music with Will. We were like a budget version of Eddie Condon and Eddie Lang. He'd 'chug' and I would 'twiddle' (playing four-beat swing and improvising

Right: Author Will Grove-White and his mentor George Hinchliffe strum tunes with Ian Whitcomb at home in London in 1990.

solos). We both had a taste for 'froth-blowing jazz' in those days, though neither of us drank much beer. Well, I didn't, anyway.

At this point I must have gone mad. I invited Will to join the orchestra for some engagements. His very first gig with us was on live TV with Ronnie Spector, and he was rather anxious. After all, millions of people would see the show. What if he made a mistake? Apparently I told him that it didn't matter, because after 30 seconds millions of people would have forgotten all about it. In any event, something changed as a result of that performance (or perhaps it was our Zen approach to it) - his confidence soared. Will hasn't been troubled by performance anxiety since. Similarly, it took us a while to get him to make musical suggestions or to sing - I always like to encourage my colleagues - but once he did start, the only snag was that it became impossible to shut him up! He still won't shut up. He's always coming up with ideas. And singing. Shut up, Will. Why don't you write a book or something?

In order to become a professional uke player and the author of this book, Will chased me down, slogged across town to the top rooms of pubs and skipped after-school activities. He missed out on holidays to gig relentlessly in village halls. He bore the vicissitudes of touring life; the cheap accommodation, the variable pay, the cheating promoters and the voracious audiences who let you know when they don't like it. He learned the hard way how to make the audience happy, from being silly to juggling ukuleles. In short, he always demonstrated a dogged determination to be exactly who he is. This is what makes Will's book so good; he's a member of the original and much-loved Ukulele Orchestra of Great Britain - the one that named and invented the concept - but more than that, he's an integral personality within the act, who's helped shape the style of our performance and influenced many others. He's paid his dues and knows what he's talking about when it comes to ukulele matters. Heck, he doesn't even mind if I use a plectrum!

Treasure this book, cherish it and bequeath it to your descendants. If only I'd been able to read this when I was first interested. I'd have loved it. You'll find information, inspiration and illumination here, and if it prompts you to form a different opinion, remember, that is a good thing. You're on your way to becoming a ukulele superstar.

PROLOGUE: MY UKULELE LIFE

My first memory of the ukulele is seeing one on a black-and-white television, held in the hands of that cheeky chappie George Formby. I was simultaneously repelled and attracted by the man and his music, but above all I loved the superhuman speed of his strumming, which seemed to me to be rocket-powered.

So, like the enthusiastic little fellow I was, I asked my mother to buy me a ukulele for my birthday. This she did, but she misunderstood my request and bought me not a banjo-ukulele (which Formby played - like a small banjo), but a tiny guitar-shaped ukulele instead. I was shocked and appalled. What was this? It wasn't nearly as brash and noisy as the Formby ukulele. I turned my nose up at it and I'm sorry to say that it lay gathering dust for the next few years.

Some time later, in the early 1980s, I went to see a performance by an old friend of my mother's, Ian Whitcomb (see page 38). Ian had been part of the British wave of pop acts in America during the 1960s and had enjoyed a Top Ten hit there. These days he was an author and musician, and when I saw him he was strumming through some old Irving Berlin tunes on his ukulele. I loved the songs and remembered the ukulele in my room. Spurred on by Ian, I dusted off my old *How to...* book and began what would become a lifelong relationship with the ukulele.

I got hold of some sheet music with the ukulele chord boxes written in and away I went, strumming through old Tin Pan Alley songs. Soon after that, though, my ears began to open to the more grungy sounds of Jimi Hendrix, The Velvet Underground and David Bowie. It was in 1987 that I read an article in the Sunday papers about a band called the Ukulele Orchestra of Great Britain (see pages 28-30). They sounded well worth a peek.

My mother duly took me along to the top room of a pub in Islington, The Empress of Russia. Little did I realize that what I was going to see that evening would change the course of my whole life. It was a tiny room, and the band was unlike any other I'd seen. It was great music, it was funny, they were cool - and I was completely hooked. From then on I did my best to get to every gig I could and, after hanging around enough, I began borrowing music from them and occasionally popping over to one of their houses for a strum-through. I even began reimagining some tunes of my own with a few pals I'd converted to the ukulele at school.

What followed was a ukulele-obsessed few years, and Ian Whitcomb was so pleased to hear he'd inspired me to play that he lent me one of his beautiful vintage Martin ukuleles. It was a real beauty and sounded out of this

world. Unfortunately, we were soon to be parted, when I fell asleep on the London Underground, the precious Martin ukulele under my seat. I awoke suddenly at my station and dashed out of the closing doors. Argh! Yes, I'd left the ukulele behind. I chased the train down the platform, banging on the glass and pointing like a madman, but the uke was gone, never to be seen again.

So, armed with a new ukulele, my next step was to join a ukulele society. There was a George Formby Society, which held meetings in Blackpool, but of course Formby played the banjo-ukulele - a noisier, frying-pan-shaped ukulele. For those of us living in the South of England, there was another group, called the Ukulele Society of Great Britain, which met at Digswell Village Hall near Welwyn Garden City, just outside London. I went there in 1986 with my mother and a smattering of members from the Ukulele Orchestra of Great Britain, and it was a wonderfully British event. Packed into this tiny hall were all manner of ukulele players. I remember an old fellow performing a dirty version of 'Are You Lonesome Tonight?' (next lines: 'Are your knickers too tight? / Is your brass-i-ere falling apart?'), and naturally there were a fair few Formby impersonators in attendance.

There were also a good number of serious ukulele players there, though, who were beginning to use the ukulele in a way I'd rarely heard before - as a purely melodious solo instrument, picked and plucked like a classical guitar. Of course, among all of this was the Ukulele Orchestra of Great Britain, totally unlike anyone else there - this bunch of cool dudes up from London playing Rolling Stones and Charlie Parker tunes. They were well received, if not totally understood, but in my eyes they could do no wrong.

Perhaps an unlikely member of the Ukulele Society was Beatle George Harrison, who often came along to the meetings. Although I never saw him there, he did meet some of the Ukulele Orchestra at a Digswell gathering and invited them back to his place for a strum. He was, by all accounts, a charming man with an unhealthy interest in ukuleles.

After a lesson in how to execute the triple stroke from phonofiddle player extraordinaire Jim Thorogood, it was time for me to leave my first ukulele convention, but I'll never forget my initiation into the eccentric world of ukulele-fanciers.

It wasn't long after this that I got a phone call asking if I'd like to play a concert with the Ukulele Orchestra. My persistent interest in them had finally paid off. The gig was on *Pebble Mill at One*, at the BBC in Birmingham. For me, it was about the most exciting thing that could happen. After wrangling with a supremely unimaginative headmaster, and even a letter to him from the Orchestra's founder George Hinchliffe explaining that I was needed, I bunked off school by calling in sick and took the train to begin what would be the rest of my life.

For many years afterwards, we played gigs at Cecil Sharp House (the home of the English Folk Dance and Song Society in Camden Town) and venues around London, as well as doing the odd tour of Japan (1994 and 2004), where we were pursued through the streets by ukulele-mad fans. Since then, the Ukulele Orchestra of Great Britain hasn't looked back, and what once seemed like a little sideline to my life ('the band I'd pay to be in,' as I used to, and still do, call it) has completely taken it over. We've played sell-out shows at the Royal Albert Hall, Carnegie Hall and the Sydney Opera House, and even done a gig at the North Pole.

Over the years I've been playing, the ukulele has been through a radical transformation. Originally the ultimate outsider instrument, it has nearly become a respected player in the musical establishment. How this happened it's hard to say, but it was certainly something to do with the Ukulele Orchestra of Great Britain, and some other wonderful ukulele performers, such as Jake Shimabukuro (see page 35) and Israel Kamakawiwo'ole (see page 32). Mix them up with the internet and a growing sense among people that small is beautiful and you have some potent ingredients for a musical revolution.

But however the renaissance of this little instrument might have occurred, there can only be a few people in the world for whom the humble ukulele manages to put food on the table, and I'm extremely proud to be among that number.

INTRODUCING THE UKULELE

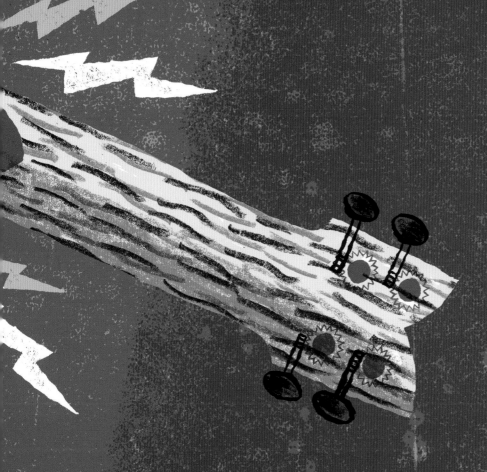

MEET THE UKULELE

The ukulele: a noble little instrument; an irritating little instrument. Both views are valid, but for millions of people around the world, the ukulele is fast becoming an instrument of desire. From China to Alaska, a revolution in music is happening under our noses, and its weapon of choice is a vertically challenged guitar.

So what is it about the humble ukulele that people find so appealing? Is it a reaction against the high-tech world we're all living in? Perhaps we can no longer afford pianos and trombones. Or maybe we just don't want to play 'normal' instruments any more.

The truth is, the ukulele is the perfect outsider instrument, one for musical misfits everywhere. If you'd prefer to forge new musical paths instead of trying to fit into an already existing hierarchy, then the uke's for you. And the aspiring plucker will often find they have an immediate affinity with the ukulele - there can be no doubt that it's a comforting instrument to hold, rather like a little sleeping baby (only be careful not to wake it).

For me, the beauty of the ukulele is that it's for everybody, with no elitist connotations. It's quick to learn, inexpensive to buy and one of the most portable instruments you can find (plus it makes a surprisingly acceptable ping-pong bat). Sitting outside the worlds of classical and modern pop music, it's the outlaw of instruments, and provides the perfect route to rebellious creative expression.

That's not to say that the ukulele doesn't have its own rich history. A distant relative of the renaissance guitar, and embedded in the folk traditions of Portugal and Hawaii, it's gone

Opposite: Johnny Marvin, aka 'The Ukulele Ace', wearing a ukulele necklace - a neat storage solution for when your ukulele collection gets out of control.

on from there to have a massive cultural impact in America, Great Britain, Japan and Canada. These days it continues on its journey towards world domination, with ukulele groups, clubs and festivals popping up in every country around the globe.

The ukulele's influence in mainstream pop and rock music has been very well hushed up. Many great artists got their first taste of music on the ukulele. Jimi Hendrix, David Byrne, David Bowie, Joe Strummer, Brian May and Joni Mitchell - to name but a few (see pages 60-83) - all started out playing the ukulele (the fact that they all moved on to another, more overgrown stringed instrument is something we will gloss over for the time being, so as not to hurt the ukulele's feelings). Even iconic figures like the first man on the moon Neil Armstrong (see pages 66-7), the blonde bombshell Marilyn Monroe (see page 80) and the king of rock 'n' roll Elvis Presley (see page 62) all enjoyed a strum to begin their day.

The ukulele has a lot going for it, but before we can even think about learning how to play it, we must first concentrate hard and learn the RULES of ukulele:

1. Music is about invention and expression, not being tied to lists of rules telling the student what is and isn't allowed.
2. That's it.

The idea of this book is to convert you into a ukulele-headed person. We'll find out about where the ukulele came from, where it's going, who got good at it, why they bothered and what all this even means. More importantly, it'll get you playing and enjoying the ukulele without all the bother of having to learn much. You'll have to practise, of course, but the ukulele is quickly rewarding, and once you've mastered the basics, the world will be your oyster - you and your miniature wooden companion can venture forth knowing that you will be welcomed with open arms wherever you go (and meet with an occasional slammed door).

When I started to learn the ukulele, in about 1985, I studied a short pamphlet with the title *How to Play the Ukulele*. It certainly looked pretty easy, and a few days later I was strumming through 'Oh! Susanna' like a pro. These days, unfortunately, there are all too many books that over-complicate the ukulele, and in doing so, they put people off. This is not one of those books.

The most important thing to know about music, and learning how to play music, is that it should be fun. From this point of view, the ukulele is the perfect instrument to get started on: if you approach it in the right frame of mind, you'll make fast progress, and very soon you'll be strumming some groovy tunes. We must tread carefully, though. The ukulele comes with a certain amount of baggage. You must always be on your guard, because:

☞ The ukulele can lead to an interest in other instruments.

☞ There is no such thing as owning just one ukulele.

☞ People will want you to play songs by George Formby (see pages 24-7) and Tiny Tim (see pages 22-4).

☞ The ukulele is irrepressibly cheerful, and sometimes you don't want to be cheerful.

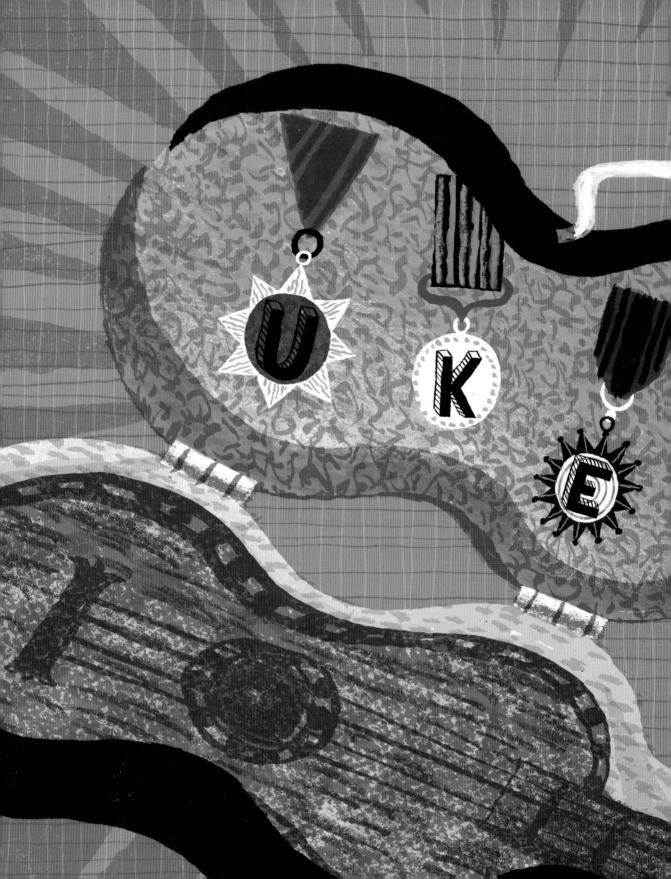

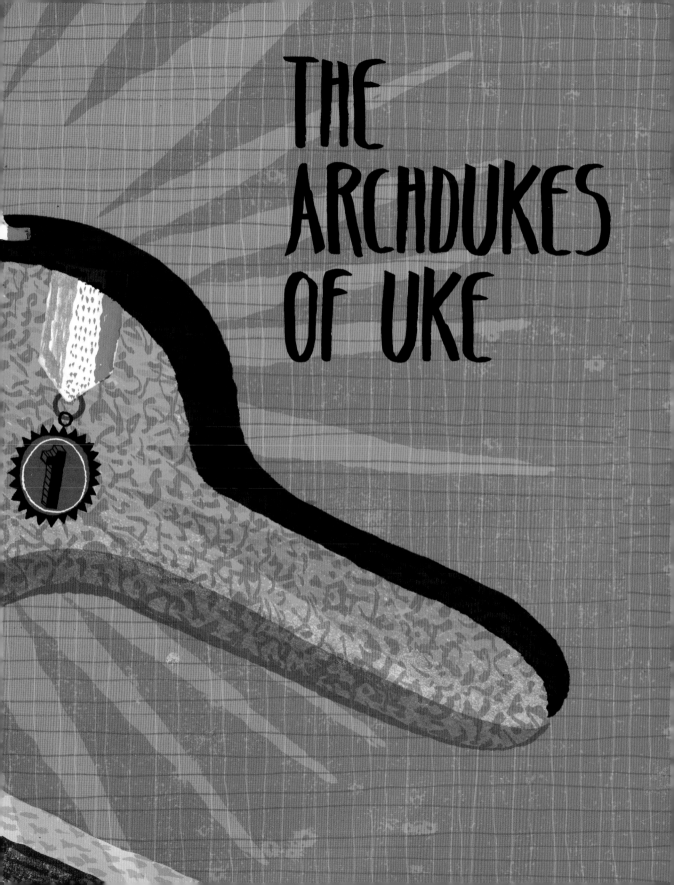

UKULELE HEROES

As the ukulele has mostly been viewed as an oddity of an instrument, sitting apart from more socially accepted ones like guitars and pianos, any artist who has made it their life's work to carve out a career playing a ukulele deserves to be loudly applauded. Even though the ukulele is currently enjoying something of a revival, it's still only on rare occasions that our tiny friend makes it into a hit song or TV show without being presented alongside a pair of raised eyebrows.

Before anyone starts complaining that I've left out their favourite ukulele player or crying how could I have included so-and-so, I'd like to point out that the following ukulele players are *my* favourites, so don't get your knickers in a twist if yours aren't represented here. Some ukulele players can't stand Tiny Tim (I, for one, love him), while others rave about the technique of more 'serious' ukulele artists. Whatever your opinion, someone can always be found who will shout the opposite. The important thing to remember is that in the world of the ukulele, it's just a matter of taste.

It's thanks to all these artists that the ukulele is doing so well today - each of them has fallen in love with the ukulele, and the public has, in turn, fallen for them.

CLIFF EDWARDS ('UKULELE IKE') 1895-1971

If I had to pick my favourite ukulele player, it would be Cliff Edwards, better known as 'Ukulele Ike'. He was a true original of his time, a sweet-talking, high-squawking, hard-drinking, red-hot ukulele player. The minute you listen to a Cliff Edwards recording, you realize his star quality: he has the voice of an angel one second, and sounds like a demented chicken the next. It's hard to imagine how he makes the noises he does, and to believe that

Opposite and above: Among Edwards's fans are cartoonist Robert Crumb, who designed this LP reissue, and Joe Brown, who played 'I'll See You In My Dreams' on a uke at George Harrison's memorial concert in 2002. It brought the house down.

seek fame in vaudeville. It was only when he moved to Chicago in 1917 that he first laid his hands on a ukulele. He bought a cheap Martin soprano, taught himself a few chords and in no time had a recording contract with Pathé, merrily scatting his way through songs such as 'I'll See You in My Dreams,' accompanying himself with some nimble strumming.

A star at the peak of the ukulele craze in America, his big break came in 1924 when he performed the first ever rendition of George and Ira Gershwin's 'Fascinatin' Rhythm' on Broadway. His wide appeal and commercial success was key to the rise in popularity of the ukulele itself.

These days he's probably best known as the chirpy voice of Jiminy Cricket in the 1940 Walt Disney film *Pinocchio*, and the singer of what would go on to become the Disney Corporation's signature tune, 'When You Wish Upon a Star'. But like so many great stars, he burned the candle at both ends. Prior to his work with Disney, Cliff's private life was in disarray, and thanks to expensive divorces and child-support demands, coupled with his penchant for booze and the good times, he filed for bankruptcy.

His luck changed for a while with the success of his Disney work, but his destructive ways were never far away. What's more, fashions were fast evolving, Cliff had lost his youthful good looks and the ukulele was no longer as popular as it had once been. After filing twice more for bankruptcy, he went into a convalescent hospital, where he died on 17 July 1971, neglected and unloved. Tragically, his body lay unclaimed for four days until he was buried by the Actors Fund of America in Valhalla Memorial Park Cemetery in Hollywood.

Who said the uke was a cheerful instrument?

they all emanate from the same person. If you've not heard him before, have a listen. I guarantee you'll be captivated.

These days he's a largely forgotten character, but in the ukulele's heyday of the 1920s, Cliff Edwards was one of the most popular singers in America, selling over 70 million records and appearing in more than 100 movies. Cliff was born in 1895 to humble beginnings in Missouri and left home at 14 to

Tiny Tim shows us how it's done. Crashing through the tulips in 1975.

TINY TIM 1933-1996

At 6ft 1in (185cm) tall, with a face covered in white make-up, tangled ringlets of black hair, a Fagin-esque nose and wonky teeth, Tiny Tim has to be one of the world's most unlikely pop stars: an asexual, falsetto-voiced oddball, devoutly religious, who sang old vaudeville and Tin Pan Alley songs accompanied by his ukulele. He was the real thing, a performer who did it because he loved it, a total one-off eccentric. There's never been anyone quite like Tiny Tim.

He was born Herbert Khaury in 1933 to a Lebanese sweater-knitting father and Jewish dressmaker mother in Manhattan. It was after a bout of appendicitis that he shut himself in his room and began listening to his father's 78rpm record collection. So began his obsession with vintage jazz and pop music of the early 1900s. By his own admission, he went on to scour shops and libraries for 78rpm records and sheet music 'like a vampire sucking blood', and his knowledge of the music of this era was encyclopedic.

Inspired by TV's Arthur Godfrey, he taught himself to play ukulele on a plastic Maccaferri Islander and would perform in any venue that would have him, from cafés to flea circuses. His persistence paid off and soon he was enjoying a cult following among the Greenwich Village groovies of the 1960s. He met Jimi Hendrix, Allen Ginsberg and Donovan, performed a private gig for Mick Jagger, hung out with Janis Joplin and was very close to Jim Morrison (who offered Tiny his song 'People are Strange').

His big break came when he appeared on a major TV show, *Rowan & Martin's Laugh-In*. At the time, no one could put their finger on exactly why, but at 36 years old, Tiny Tim became an overnight sensation. Appearances followed on *The Tonight Show Starring Johnny Carson* and he quickly signed a record deal. He released the album *God Bless Tiny Tim* in 1968. 'Tiptoe Through the Tulips' became his biggest hit, selling over 200,000 copies. That same year Tiny played a sensational sell-out gig at the Royal Albert Hall in London (attended by Elton John, The Beatles, The Rolling Stones and my mum).

He released another two albums, and went on to marry his girlfriend, the 17-year-old Miss Vicki, on *The Tonight Show*, an event that broke TV viewing records of the time. Miss Vicki later claimed that it was an unhappy union, telling the *Daily Mirror* in 1974 that Tiny chose to sleep 'alone in his own bed in thick woollen pyjamas'.

Even in the late 1970s, when the wider public had largely forgotten about him, Tiny was at his happiest on stage, whether performing in a Travelodge hotel or doing a private gig for some random fan. He remained a consummate professional, always taking time out for his supporters, even when it meant signing huge piles of old sheet music after a show.

The constant touring and performances eventually took their toll, though, and in 1996 Tiny Tim had a heart attack at a Massachusetts ukulele festival. He recovered, but against medical advice he kept performing, and two months later he had a fatal heart attack while singing 'Tiptoe Through the Tulips' in Minneapolis. What a way to go.

BOB DYLAN AND TINY TIM

In Bob Dylan's memoirs he writes how after he arrived in New York in 1961, he and Tiny would hang out together at the Café Wha?, both up-and-coming artists in Greenwich Village, begging food from the cook.

When working on the famous *Basement Tapes* with The Band, Robbie Robertson was raving to Dylan about Tiny Tim, whom Dylan of course remembered well. They were thinking of making a film at the time and so they got Tiny down to their studio in Woodstock, where they recorded some tunes. Dylan filmed lots of footage with Tiny, but it's never been seen.

At this time the two of them spent what must have been one of the more surreal evenings of the 1960s together. Tiny Tim sang 'Like a Rolling Stone' to Dylan, but in the style of 1930s crooner Rudy Vallée. He then proceeded to serenade him with Vallée's 'My Time Is Your Time' in the style of Bob Dylan. In Tiny's account, Dylan was speechless and could only manage to say, 'Look, do you want a banana before you go to bed?'

Tiny politely replied, 'No, Mr Dylan, I have my own fruit with me', and retired.

Opposite: George gives the troops a laugh in Normandy, France in 1944. His wife, Beryl, sits beside him holding his uke case.

GEORGE FORMBY 1904–1961

Born in 1904 in Wigan, Lancashire, in the coal-mining North of England, George Formby is the character that most divides British ukulele players. For some, he's nothing more than a politically incorrect, banjo-wielding, tinny-voiced irritation. For others, he represents the best of British; a cheeky northerner, never without a nudge and a wink - the underdog who always came out on top with his ukulele.

Whatever your view of George, there's no underestimating his impact on British culture. In his day, Formby was the best-known and highest-paid performer in Britain. He had a 40-year career, starred in 21 hit films and released over 230 records. While his songs were full of double entendre, his apparently innocent personality and cheerful winks and nods to the audience belied the naughty lyrics.

'I've got a picture of a nudist camp, in my
    little snapshot album,
All very jolly but a trifle damp, in my little
    snapshot album,
There's Uncle Dick without a care,
Discarding all his underwear,
But his watch and chain still dangle there,
    in my little snapshot album.'

His 1937 song 'With My Little Stick of Blackpool Rock' (fnar, fnar) was banned by the BBC because of its suggestive lyrics - an honour he shares with the Sex Pistols, I'm sure he'd be tickled to know. The BBC also banned 'With My Little Ukulele in My Hand', and his biggest hit, 'When I'm Cleaning Windows', but this did little to diminish the public's appetite - sales leapt to 200,000 a month.

Quite apart from his skill as a performer and singer (he has a rather sweet voice when he gets the chance to show it off), George Formby was a

The Archdukes of Uke 25

great ukulele player. He was a bit of a one-trick pony, but he did that trick better than anyone else. His style of strumming (a super-charged combination of the split stroke and the triple stroke [see page 148]) is now known as the 'Formby style,' and his songs would commonly feature a blistering ukulele solo as he strummed himself into a frenzy. Although his right-hand technique was something special, he only knew a few chord shapes, so he carried a variety of different ukuleles, all tuned in different keys, so he could use the same tricks in any song he wanted to play.

His musical act was based around that of his late father. George Formby Senior had been a famous music-hall actor and comedian, and,

when he died on stage in 1921, George Junior abandoned an unhappy career as a jockey to take up where his father had left off. Initially, George was a flop on stage, but his fortunes rapidly changed once he met his ambitious future wife, ex-clog-dancing champion Beryl Ingham. She would go on to be the powerhouse behind George's success, managing his finances, organizing his shows and choosing his songs. It's even said that at the end of George's live shows, she'd appear from the side of the stage and take the bows alongside him.

Throughout the Second World War, George tirelessly entertained the troops. He was the first performer to go to France, and the last to leave when the British evacuated, with Beryl always at his side. After the war, Beryl and George toured South Africa, just before apartheid was introduced. They refused to play segregated venues, and when they were cheered at a concert for hugging a small black girl, Daniel Malan, the head of the ultra-right National Party, called to complain. Beryl didn't mince her words, saying, 'Why don't you **** off, you horrible little man.'

When George died, at 56 years old, over 100,000 mourners lined the streets for his funeral in Warrington, Cheshire. By then he was a national treasure, who had put the ukulele squarely on the map as the instrument of the underdog. George's legacy lives on today in the George Formby Society, whose annual get-together in Blackpool attracts hundreds of fans, and whose membership has included George Harrison.

Opposite: George demonstrates the attractive powers of the ukulele, looking like all his Christmases have come at once.

UKULELE ORCHESTRA OF GREAT BRITAIN 1985-

The group that's done the most to popularize the ukulele around the world over the last 25 years has to be the Ukulele Orchestra of Great Britain. The world's very first Ukulele Orchestra, they've gone on to spawn hundreds of ukulele groups across the globe and are seen in Britain as something of a national institution, in the great tradition of variety entertainers. A group of eight singer-strummers, their approach to music is built on the premise that 'all genres of music are available for reinterpretation, as long as they are played on the ukulele'.

The UOGB began plucking together in 1985, when the ukulele in Britain was a forgotten instrument, its only association being the grinning Mr Formby. Since then they've had a remarkable journey, from small gigs in the backrooms of London pubs to sold-out performances in world-renowned concert halls.

The Orchestra is the brainchild of Sheffield-born multi-instrumentalist and musicologist George Hinchliffe. After musical beginnings arranging tunes for fairground organs, as well as playing the Hammond organ with visiting US soul artists like Martha Reeves and Ben E King, he moved to London where he rediscovered the ukulele, which he'd played as a child. After years of lugging a Hammond organ from gig

to gig, the Smurf ukulele that he found himself strumming at Richie Williams's house made a welcome change. As he explained, 'The limited palette of the ukulele was very appealing, like a pencil drawing versus an oil painting. In the right hands, a pencil can still produce an amazing work of art; it just presents different challenges. Take a look at Picasso or Dürer.'

Along with George's college friends Kitty Lux and Andy Astle, he assembled a group of performers and musicians and formed the UOGB for what was supposed to be a one-off gig at The Roebuck pub in Southwark, London. 'I wanted the band to be like the Amadeus Quartet, Benny Goodman's big band and The Rolling Stones rolled into one.' The Orchestra was an immediate

Below: The UOGB line-up (left to right), Dave Suich, Peter Brooke Turner, Hester Goodman, George Hinchliffe, Richie Williams, Kitty Lux, Will Grove-White and Jonty Bankes.

....

hit, with the *NME* writing: 'Most people have to die before they become immortal. These ukulele superstars have no such worries.' They booked more gigs and over the next three years released an LP, recorded a BBC Radio 1 session, performed at the WOMAD festival and in America.

Since those early days, this self-run organization has played gigs across the globe, from Svalbard in the Arctic Circle to Australia and New Zealand via North America, Europe, China and Japan - sixteen-handedly changing the way that audiences think about the ukulele.

Their sell-out Royal Albert Hall concert at the BBC Proms in 2008 was attended by over six thousand people, more than a thousand of whom brought their ukuleles along to join the UOGB in a rendition of Beethoven's 'Ode to Joy'. This iconic ukulele event was quickly followed by concerts at New York's Carnegie Hall in 2010 and 2012, and the Sydney Opera House in 2012, as well as collaborations with Madness, Kaiser Chiefs, Cat Stevens, Robbie Williams and Ibiza DJs.

Dressed in black dinner suits, just like a 'proper' orchestra, the group's gigs can feature versions of anything from Ennio Morricone's theme from *The Good, the Bad and the Ugly* to Nirvana's 'Smells Like Teen Spirit', via Tchaikovsky and Isaac Hayes. While they take a light-hearted approach to performance, they

Above: A mass ukulele salute at the BBC Proms in 2008 - there were enough ukes in attendance to build an impressive bonfire.

are serious about music, and their repertoire often reveals beauty in unexpected places. Stripping popular music down to its ukulele bones can move an audience in unexpected ways as they hear the music and lyrics anew.

There's no doubt that the ukulele has come a long way in the past 30 years. George Hinchliffe says, 'When I think back to the early days, people were generally into the ukulele in one of two ways - Formby or Hawaiian. If you tried to play anything else, it was seen as "wrong", and people could get surprisingly aggressive about it. Thank goodness that nowadays nobody cares much - you can play what you like.' And long may they keep doing just that.

TESSIE O'SHEA 1913-1995

Tessie O'Shea was a huge, spellbinding, show-stopping superstar - Wales's very own answer to George Formby. Born in Cardiff in 1913, she was big in all senses: her voice, her body, her vitality and her showmanship. As well as singing and acting, she played the banjo-ukulele like a demon and managed to give Formby a real run for his money in the strumming stakes. She was a star of the stage in Britain and later in America as well (where she was eventually to settle down), stealing the show on Broadway in Noël Coward's *The Girl Who Came to Supper*.

A marvellous clip that still exists (find it on YouTube) shows her appearance on *The Ed Sullivan Show* in 1964. To see Tessie perform 'Two Ton Tessie from Tennessee' is to look directly into the best of British music hall, so effortlessly does she captivate her audience. She positively glides onto the stage (wrapped in ermine) and proceeds to ooze show business in a whirlwind six minutes of pure energy. This was no mean feat, because the other act appearing on *The Ed Sullivan Show* that night was none other than The Beatles, at the height of their powers.

It's a shame that it's remembered as the Liverpudlians' episode, because not only did she do such a great job, but The Beatles themselves were great fans of Tessie's (especially John Lennon). I can just imagine George Harrison buttonholing her backstage

Above: Tessie and The Beatles in 1964. She would sign this photo, 'from Tessie O'Shea and her favourite boys'.

about all matters ukulele, preferring to enquire about her triple-stroke technique (see page 148) rather than face the thousands of screaming fans waiting for them.

ISRAEL KAMAKAWIWO'OLE 1959-1997

Israel was, in more ways than one, a giant of recent Hawaiian music, and a hell-raiser of the ukulele scene. A colossal figure, weighing in at over 50 stone (317.5kg) and standing an impressive 6ft 2in (1.88m) tall, his little ukulele positively vanished in his huge embrace.

In contrast to his imposing presence, he had a beautifully soft and gentle voice, which he used to great effect on what became his most famous recording, a medley of 'Somewhere Over the Rainbow' and 'What a Wonderful World', released in 1993. It's a silky-smooth and laid-back reworking of these classic tunes, which appears on *Facing Future*, his most famous album. When it went platinum, it was the first Hawaiian album ever to do so, and put Hawaiian music firmly back on the worldwide map.

Israel was a renegade character from his earliest years, and although this earned him a reputation as a man of the people, it wasn't long before he was overindulging himself in drugs and alcohol, as well as food. His sheer enormity meant that even getting him to gigs became a logistical nightmare, requiring oxygen tanks and teams of helpers. Although he later renounced drugs, his addictive ways were to be his downfall. He died at only 38 years old, due to his obesity, and the Hawaii state flags flew at half-mast on the day of his funeral. Thousands of people paid their respects as his ashes were scattered into the Pacific Ocean.

With the unfortunate yet inevitable westernization of Hawaiian culture, Israel must have been a breath of fresh air to native Hawaiians - he was passionate about traditional Hawaiian language (which he learned to speak), and a dedicated champion of Hawaiian independence and the rights of the indigenous people. His importance in reinvigorating the Hawaiian ukulele scene can't be underestimated.

Left: Israel offering proof to any doubters that you don't need little fingers to play the ukulele.

MAY SINGHI BREEN 1895-1970

May Singhi Breen was a genuine ukulele freedom fighter. A New Yorker, married to pianist Peter De Rose, she did more than most to further the cause of our humble little friend and richly deserves her moniker, 'The Ukulele Lady'.

She was first given a ukulele as a Christmas present, and after unsuccessfully trying to exchange it for a bathrobe (as many after her would try to do), May thought she might as well give the uke a go. It was a good job she did, because she went on to become a major ukulele celebrity in the 1920s and 1930s. She even had her own radio show, through which she spread the ukulele bug far and wide, wrote her own ukulele tutor book and recorded the world's first ever ukulele lesson on a 78rpm record.

More than this, May was one of the first to recognize the huge market for ukuleles. Ever since the boom in recorded music and the mass production of gramophones, more people were listening to music, but fewer people were taking up 'difficult' instruments like the piano - they could hear the original tunes on their record players. Seeing the commercial potential of the easy-to-play uke, May single-handedly persuaded Tin Pan Alley music publishers to print ukulele chord boxes on their sheet music. Now, anybody with a ukulele could lead a sing-a-long of any popular tune. This has to be one of the biggest contributions to ukulele history - look at almost any sheet music from this era and you'll see the ukulele chord boxes on it, more often than not arranged by May Singhi Breen herself.

Above: The Ukulele Lady poses with converts at her long-running NBC radio show 'Sweethearts of the Air'.

Not content to leave it at that, she next locked horns with the American Federation of Musicians. Horrified to find that she'd been refused membership on the grounds that the ukulele was merely a novelty instrument, May made it a personal crusade to get the ukulele recognized as a bona fide musical instrument, bombarding them with applications. After years of wrangling, combined with pressure from two other ukulele-playing stars of the day, Cliff Edwards and Arthur Godfrey, the Federation finally relented. So it is that nowadays ukulele players can proudly stand shoulder to shoulder with harmonica players, recorder players, triangle players and other 'proper' musicians.

LAURA DUKES 1907-1992 AND CHARLIE BURSE, AKA 'UKULELE KID', 1901-1965

While watching a BBC music documentary about the blues from 1976 (*The Devil's Music – A History of the Blues*), I was surprised to see a remarkable old lady perched on the edge of a bed, hollering out an old country song entitled 'Crawdad' on a ukulele. She played simple, strong, on-the-beat ukulele throughout, and sang with a voice that had obviously travelled the length and breadth of America. She was Laura Dukes.

Born in Memphis in 1907, her father had been the drummer in W C Handy's band (the 'Father of the Blues'), and it wasn't long before Laura was giving her first performance, singing 'Balling the Jack' on stage at only five years old. She'd go on performing across the American South until the end of her life, but would become best known as a singer and ukulele player.

While dancing and singing at minstrel shows, Laura learned to play music on the hoof, taught mostly by guitarist Robert Nighthawk. She loved the ukulele, and when she arrived in East St Louis, Illinois, she took the plunge. 'That's when I bought a banjo-ukulele', she said, 'I always did like a small instrument, you know, with four strings.' At only 4ft 7in (140cm) tall, she must have suited the ukulele down to the ground.

In the 1930s she recorded with the historic Memphis Jug Band. She later remembered life in the famous Beale Street well: 'We went in the Gray Mule, Pee Wee's Saloon and so many places...I done forgot. I would go around with Ukulele Kid and Will Shade.' Wait a minute - the Ukulele Kid? Who was he?

One of the only ukulele bluesmen of his time, 'Ukulele Kid' was Charlie Burse, a man renowned for both his ferocious temper and his uke skills. There still exists a delightful clip of him playing a baritone ukulele (or a tenor guitar, for the pedants out there) accompanied by Will Shade on washtub bass. He went on to write some fantastic tunes with his own band, the Memphis Mudcats, including the appetizing 'Too Much Beef' and the interestingly titled 'Weed Smoking Mama'. He was also a key influence on the young Elvis Presley (see page 62), who would come to watch him perform on Beale Street.

Laura went on to record and play with the Will Batts Novelty Band, but just like the Ukulele Kid, she was playing smaller and smaller venues by the 1950s. Unfortunately, the Ukulele Kid died in 1965, before the rekindling of interest in the blues that would revive so many careers. Laura, though, kept performing right up until the 1980s, still strumming her heart out, when she became something of a favourite among the new generation of blues fans.

Above top: Laura Dukes puts a plastic ukulele through its paces. Above bottom: Charlie Burse plucking away in full jug band mode.

JAKE SHIMABUKURO 1976-

Jake Shimabukuro has been strumming the ukulele since he was four years old, encouraged by his mother, who also plays. Since then, he's certainly been putting the practice in. After playing in bands at school, he went on to release his own ukulele albums in Japan and Hawaii. It was in 2006, though, that he was to become a megastar on the worldwide ukulele stage. He performed a version of The Beatles' 'While My Guitar Gently Weeps' in New York's Central Park for a great website (now sadly defunct) called Midnight Ukulele Disco. The short video clip was uploaded to YouTube and went viral, sending Jake on a seemingly never-ending tour of America.

A modern-day Hawaiian ukulele player, he's a technical virtuoso, playing blisteringly fast riffs and strums at his solo concerts. He even performed at the 2009 Royal Variety Performance in London accompanying Bette Midler, and *Guitar Player* magazine went so far as to call him the 'Jimi Hendrix of the ukulele' (a title that leads one to wonder who the George Formby of the guitar might be...).

He's one contemporary artist who's made the ukulele do something new, transforming its sound - to me it sounds something like a harp crossed with a celeste. In a way, his great skill means that his ukulele no longer sounds like a ukulele, which seems a bit of a shame, but happily that leaves the tuneless plunking to the rest of us. If you're concerned with technical virtuosity, you're probably more likely to want to give up the ukulele than start after seeing him play, but he's a great talent, a nice chap and worth checking out.

Right: Although Mr Shimabukuro strikes Townshend-esque power chords, he won't smash up his uke at the end of the show.

Another expert player (like Jake Shimabukuro), he's technically incredibly accomplished, but also takes great delight in getting all sorts of unexpected sounds out of his ukulele. He'll use it as a drum while playing the tune and chords at the same time (a kind of plate-spinning for ukuleles - you boggle at his ability to keep all the parts going), and also does a very nice line in chopstick ukulele playing (bashing and scraping the strings with the sticks to create an array of surprising sounds). 'People say the ukulele is a toy. I used to resent that. Now I don't mind it…I mean, what's wrong with toys?' His version of Michael Jackson's 'Billie Jean' is well worth a look on YouTube, as are his recent rootsy collaborations with cellist Anne Janelle.

Above: James Hill is a great ambassador for the instrument, teaching uke workshops and sharing tips wherever he goes.

JAMES HILL 1980-

Canadian James Hill learned the ukulele at school in British Columbia. Thanks to an innovative music teacher - the marvellously goateed J Chalmers Doane - the ukulele had become a staple of musical education throughout British Columbia during the 1970s and 1980s, and James Hill was one of those to benefit. He told me, 'The uke helped me to make friends whether I liked it or not. As an introvert, it was a blessing in disguise.'

UKULELE AFTERNOON 1990-

After the Ukulele Orchestra of Great Britain, Japanese art-rock outfit Ukulele Afternoon are my favourite ukulele group. Formed in 1990 in reaction to Japan's heavily Hawaii-biased ukulele scene, they're an ever-changing group of like-minded players. They encourage anyone with a ukulele to join them in their monthly madcap rehearsals in Tokyo's Yoyogi Park, and often embark on 'guerilla' street performances, gathering in busy public spaces where they whip out their ukuleles and launch into joyful versions of tunes like 'Twist and Shout' or 'Tequila'.

Over the years they've had more than three hundred members, but a strong core have been there throughout. Mochy, (the MC, conductor and vibe controller), Oda (the groove master)

Above: Ukulele Afternoon relax in full Japanese garb in Asakusa, Tokyo, in 2013. The tiny ukulele is big in Japan.

and Miox (the virtuosic musical director) have ensured that Ukulele Afternoon stays crazy, positive, artistic and distinctly Japanese.

With between 10 and 25 members performing in their live stage shows, the sound they make is remarkably refreshing for a ukulele group. This is largely because nearly all of the members play the melody line, while only one or two strum the chords. This is the opposite of what most all-ukulele groups do (where there are usually heaps of strummers and one person plucking a tune). By arranging pieces in this way, Ukulele Afternoon create a charming and unmistakable sound that I defy anyone not to fall for.

IAN WHITCOMB 1941-

In 1960s America, only a handful of people braved playing the ukulele in public, so low had opinion of the instrument sunk. Tiny Tim was one of them, but before him came Ian Whitcomb, an eccentric Englishman who had a US Top Ten hit in 1965 with 'You Turn Me On'.

Ian travelled to America as part of the British pop invasion of the 1960s, and while his chart success led to appearances on *Shindig!* and *American Bandstand*, and won him hordes of screaming teenage fans, secretly he led a double life as a ukulele player. In 1963, Ian bought a Martin ukulele on a whim from a pawnshop in Los Angeles and immediately fell in love with it. Even performances at the Hollywood Bowl with The Beach Boys and tours with The Rolling Stones and The Kinks couldn't dim his off-stage strumming habit.

After encouragement from surf band The Turtles, Ian released his first ukulele-based single, the 1916 comedy tune 'Where Did Robinson Crusoe Go With Friday on Saturday Night?' It was certainly something of a gamble when you bear in mind that 1966 was also the year that The Beatles released 'Paperback Writer' and 'Nowhere Man', and Stevie Wonder was cooking up 'Uptight (Everything's Alright)'.

Although the single did well on the West Coast, it spelled the beginning of the end for Ian's career as a heart-throb rock 'n' roller. He told me, 'I knew I couldn't be a rock 'n' roll star for long - but when I released "Crusoe" I was no longer seen as a serious contender in the rock race. The thing was that I'd always just loved music hall, and so I began on the long march backwards into the past.'

In the 1970s, Ian started to write books about Tin Pan Alley, music hall and vaudeville, notably

After the Ball, and became a well-respected authority on the subject. He still managed to fit in the occasional ukulele-playing appearance on Johnny Carson's *Tonight Show* as well.

Ian kept digging what sometimes must have seemed a lonely furrow in the ukulele world, but his continual enthusiasm for the instrument - through his wonderful writing, records, concerts and film work - has done heaps to aid its current revival. Sadly, after a recent illness, Ian can't play much any more, but he continues to broadcast radio shows and write. I'll always be deeply grateful to him for being the one to start me on the ukulele road - and I'm still sorry about losing his Martin.

Above: Ian strums his ukulele in Hollywood in 1965, after recording 'Where Did Robinson Crusoe Go...?'

RABBIT MUSE 1908-1982

My personal favourite ukulele bluesman was the loose-limbed, droopy-eyed Lewis 'Rabbit' Muse. Born in Virginia in 1908, he took up the ukulele after watching a musician at a minstrel show. Although his attempt to stow away with the travelling performers was scuppered by his father, who called in the police, Rabbit went on to become an expert ukulele player, singer and eccentric dancer, performing his own versions of jazz, blues and country tunes, often inspired by his idol, Cab Calloway. He played a pretty mean kazoo solo as well.

Blaine Shively (who photographed Rabbit for his album covers) remembers him as a 'consummate jokester' who was always ready with a smile: 'He was a kind and gentle man. I never heard him utter a harsh word about anybody or anything.'

Someone who knew Rabbit from the days when he was a teenager performing at fairs is Bill Jefferson, a well-known local DJ and musician with the Country Playboys. Bill would often invite Rabbit to play alongside the Playboys with his ukulele on their regular TV show. On the journeys home, Bill told me, 'Rabbit'd always get in the back of the car and play the ukulele and sing all the way back home. He was a wonderful musician and a real comedian. And, boy, he could dance. He used to really tear 'em up.'

Rabbit recorded two ukulele albums, *Muse Blues* and *Sixty Minute Man*, and although they're now sadly out of print, there are some wonderful tracks up on YouTube, as well as a couple you can buy ('Rabbit Stomp' and 'Jailhouse Blues'), which I strongly urge you to chase down.

Poignantly, Rabbit and his ukulele were never to be parted. Speaking of when Rabbit died in 1982, Bill Jefferson told me: 'When I went to the funeral, they'd laid him out there with his ukulele in his hands. They buried his ukulele with him.'

Above: There's a rabbit on the grass. Rabbit relaxes behind the recording studios in Rocky Mount, Virginia in 1977. His ukulele is a 'Wendell Hall Teeviola Tenor', which Rabbit would string up with metal strings to give an unusually distinctive sound.

A HISTORY OF THE UKULELE

THE WORLD BEFORE UKES

Throughout the history of music, small plucked instruments have never been far from our sides. Whenever I look at old paintings, stained-glass windows (right) or stone carvings (below), I inevitably spot some character or other plucking a ukulele-shaped instrument. What is it about a tiny box attached to a stick with a few strings tied on it that appeals to us so much? I would guess it's because

small chordophones are people-sized (making them perfect to travel with), cheerful-sounding and easy to pick out a tune on. Whatever the reason, they seem to be part of being human.

The ukulele is always spoken of as part of the guitar family, which makes sense, because one looks like an inflated version of the other. You'll notice I didn't say that one looks like a shrunken version of the other, because it's important to realize that many of the earliest guitars had four 'courses' of paired strings - essentially four strings, just like the ukulele. The six-stringed guitar that we are all familiar with is, therefore, something of a weird modern ukulele hybrid, to which we won't give much airtime. Either way, the ukulele-type instrument came first, so there.

The first sign we see of four-stringed (or coursed) chordophones in western music are the gittern and the citole. Both appeared in Europe around the 13th century and both were endearingly small, fretted, plucked instruments. Historians debate their origins, but they're probably related to the oud, which came to Spain via the Moors, and more distantly connected to West African instruments (check out the ngoni).

Both the gittern and citole appear to have enjoyed high status among the nobility of the time, who all loved a good old knees-up to a plucked consort - and let's face it, who doesn't? The modern ukulele has also had its fair share of royal fans. Edward VIII was well known for his playing. *The Times* rather snootily noted that on a trip to South Africa in 1925, he jammed with some native musicians: 'The Prince in his saloon could be heard linking into the harmonies on his ukulele, and he delighted the simple minstrels by telling them that their people ought to be proud of their talent.' But the instrument to which the ukulele owes the greatest debt is undoubtedly the cavaquinho. This is a Portuguese instrument and the grandfather of the ukulele. In Portuguese its name translates as a small piece of firewood (from *cavaco*), which makes sense, because many is the time when a listener has wished for a box of matches while listening to some ukulele players pluck a tune.

And the place where the cavaquinho was to give birth to its son (the father of the ukulele) was in Madeira, an island in the North Atlantic that the Portuguese discovered by mistake in 1420. After the Portuguese settled in Madeira, the cavaquinho had a change of name and became known as the braguinha, and also the machete (pronounced 'ma-shet' - not to be confused with a massive sharp cleaver). These instruments became extremely popular on the island, and a great tradition of playing - sometimes solo, but often in large groups - soon developed (see picture, page 159).

At this point in the history of the ukulele, British author and mathematician Lewis Carroll makes a surprise appearance. Madeira was a popular holiday destination among wealthy 19th-century Europeans - including Henry Liddell, the Dean of Christ Church, Carroll's Oxford college. Evidently Liddell brought home some souvenirs, because in 1858 Carroll took the photo below of Liddell's daughters wearing Madeiran lace and holding machetes in their hands. Offering proof that the ukulele is the harbinger of great works of art, the girl on the left is Alice Liddell, who would go on to inspire Carroll to write *Alice's Adventures in Wonderland*. But who can say? Perhaps they are not machetes but full-size guitars, and Alice and her sisters have just eaten the growing cake...

In any case, it wouldn't be long before the machete would have its own growth spurt and spread further around the world than anyone could have expected - though this time under a more familiar name, the ukulele.

Far opposite: An early Byzantine figure plucks a tune (6th/7th century). Opposite: A heavenly uke from 1310 resides in the Cathedral of Rouen, France. Below: Alice (left) and her sisters, Lorina and Edith, pose with machetes in 1858.

TO HAWAII, WHERE THE UKULELE IS BORN

It's not often in musical history that you can pin things down to a precise date, but we know without doubt that the day the machete came to Hawaii was 23 August 1879. It arrived aboard a boat, the *Ravenscraig*, which had been carrying immigrants from Madeira to work on Hawaii's sugar plantations. The perfect instrument for sea travel, it would have fitted nicely into a tight spot, and might also have made a decent paddle in an emergency.

Ravenscraig

Among the passengers aboard this boat were two men, one with a machete (João Soares da Silva), and one without (João Fernandes). The man with the machete couldn't play it, and the man without could. Once they met, like Jack Sprat and his wife, they were a match made in heaven.

Da Silva lent his machete to Fernandes, who went on to entertain the passengers throughout their mammoth five-month voyage. It is testament to Fernandes' great musical skill that he was not thrown into a sack and tossed overboard. Indeed, when he arrived in Hawaii, still strumming, it was the turn of the Hawaiians to fall in love with the man and his funny little instrument, which they immediately did.

João Fernandes wrote that once in Hawaii he 'strummed away to his heart's content,' and the local newspaper reported with great delight the nightly street concerts that the Madeirans had been giving for the locals. It wasn't long before Fernandes and his newly formed group were giving performances at parties and balls across the island, as well as to the Hawaiian royal family, who were rapid converts to the instrument. King David Kalakaua and Queen Lili'uokalani even took to creating their own ukulele songs, the Queen composing the Hawaiian classic 'Aloha 'Oe'.

Kind David held wild and decadent parties in his $350,000 palace, with poker games, ukulele players and plenty of booze. A regular and unlikely guest at these events was Robert Louis Stevenson, author of *Treasure Island* and a renowned traveller. He loved the machete and had one of his own, which he took with him as he journeyed around the world.

It was around this time that the machete became the 'ukulele'. There are lots of theories as to why it was so named, but the most popular is that it comes from the Hawaiian words '*uku*'

Above: Robert Louis Stevenson (second left) chats to King David (far left) in 1889. Spot the uke at the back!

Amazingly, the question of how to pronounce the word 'ukulele' works some people into a right old lather. The Hawaiians traditionally pronounce it 'ooh-koo-leh-leh', and ukulele academics stress that it should be written: 'ukulele (with a Hawaiian diacritical mark at the front). Hawaiians are, rightly, very protective of their culture and prefer to hear their native instrument named in the traditional way, but many ukulele purists have made it their personal crusade to tell the rest of the world that it's wrong to pronounce it 'you-ker-lay-lee'. The truth of the matter is that the ukulele has become a worldwide phenomenon and has naturally undergone many transformations across cultures, and pronunciation is just one of them. The guitar was originally called a gittern, after all, but people still manage to keep their cool when we call it a guitar, even if it is a bit too big and noisy.

(meaning flea) and '*lele*' (which means jumping). The reason for it being identified with a flea might be to do with the size of the instrument, but some have said it was more to do with the performances of the Madeirans (who were full of beans and much smaller than the Hawaiians). I like to think that it's more to do with the nature of a flea: they are remarkable little creatures, capable of great leaps and feats of strength, but they can get a bit irritating if they get too close.

Manuel Nunes is the man most often credited with transforming the instrument from the machete into the ukulele. He started the world's first ukulele-making business, which survives in Hawaii to this day. The instruments that he and other companies began building proved so popular that by 1888 the ukulele was hailed as the national instrument of Hawaii.

HU-LA-LA

AMERICA TAKES HAWAII

(AND ITS UKULELE)

Hawaii has always held great appeal as a strategic base for America, situated as it is in the middle of the Pacific Ocean, acting as a stepping stone to the Far East. So it came as no surprise when in 1893 a group of European and US businessmen (with some gentle support from a group of US Marines) overthrew the Hawaiian monarchy in a bloodless coup.

Although Queen Lili'uokalani protested to US President Cleveland, an internal investigation by the Americans found the Marines not guilty of any involvement in the overthrow (wouldn't you have guessed it?), so Hawaii was then under US control. Many years later, in 1959, Hawaii would become America's 50th state, but not before it had seduced the country with its music and culture - and its ukulele. Over 100 years after the coup, in 2008, America would even elect its very first Hawaii-born president - Barak Obama.

Hawaii's natural beauty attracted huge numbers of visitors, and a welcome pack of flowery garlands and grass skirts was de rigueur for any tourist. It was this image of sun-drenched islanders, wreathed with flowers and strumming their ukuleles, that would become the defining image of Hawaii for generations of Americans and Europeans.

To sell Hawaii as an attractive business and cultural destination, Hawaiian musical groups - all of which featured our four-stringed friend - were despatched across America, performing at world fairs, circuses and vaudeville shows. But it was the 1915 Panama-Pacific International Exposition in San Francisco that would launch the ukulele into American popular culture. The Hawaiian Government constructed a dedicated building at the exposition, which 17 million visitors attended over nine months. There were vast tanks of exotic fish, palm trees

and tropical flowers to delight the crowds, but it was the musical performances that stole the show. A number of Hawaiian bands were drafted in to play (and did so, continuously), such as the Royal Hawaiian Quartette, led by top Hawaiian musician Keoki Awai, while hula girls wiggled enticingly. The public was spellbound.

As the *San Francisco Chronicle* would report in 1916, 'The country has all of a sudden gone mad over Hawaiian music.' The ukulele was a good-time, optimistic instrument, matching the atmosphere in America at that time. The stars had aligned; ukulele fever was about to reach its apex.

UKULELE FEVER PITCH

Suddenly all and sundry were cashing in on the new craze. To the consternation of the Hawaiians, US mainland companies began mass-producing their own ukuleles, how-to books and sheet music, while American songwriters began churning out English-language songs with a Hawaiian twist, like 'On the Beach at Waikiki' and 'They're Wearing 'em Higher in Hawaii,' as well as tunes such as Al Jolson's 'Yaaka Hula Hickey Dula,' which purported to be in Hawaiian but were really just nonsense. When a Hawaiian band leader was asked the meaning of this lyric by an American tourist, he replied, 'I'm sorry sir...I don't speak any foreign languages.'

Even the outbreak of the First World War in 1917 couldn't dim the public's appetite for ukuleles. West Coaster Isabelle Works mounted a campaign in 1918 to get a ukulele into every army tent in California. She firmly stated: 'There is nothing like a ukulele to drive the "blues" away when a boy begins to think of home and sweethearts.' When the YMCA asked the public to donate old ukuleles to the troops, they were sent in their hundreds (a little-known side-effect of the First World War is that it helped to spread the ukulele to Europe).

By the mid-1920s, over four million ukuleles were being made every year in America as the little flea moved further and further away from its Hawaiian birthplace. Companies more commonly associated with classical instruments and guitars, like Martin, Gretsch, Gibson and Lyon & Healy, all made a killing selling ukuleles, so great was the demand. Tin Pan Alley sheet music even had ukulele chord boxes printed on it as standard, thanks to the work of ukulele pioneer May Singhi Breen (see page 33). Music was being democratized and freed from written notation - anyone could play anything, as long as they had a ukulele.

It got to the point where the ukulele was so popular that only an out-of-touch celebrity would dare be seen without one. Buster Keaton, Gary Cooper, Gloria Swanson, Ramón Novarro, Harold Lloyd, Greta Garbo and Joan Crawford were all proud ukulele players and used them in publicity shots. The uke was furthering careers.

Opposite: The legendary Gloria Swanson poses in revealing (for the day) attire with her ukulele in 1916, while filming 'Sunshine'. Above: A poster for the 'Mid-Pacific Carnival' in Honolulu, featuring hula dancers, musicians and circus acts.

As time went on, America produced rafts of uke virtuosos. Roy Smeck ('The Wizard of the Strings'), Johnny Marvin ('The Ukulele Ace'), Wendell Hall ('The Red-Headed Music Maker') and the most famous player of the era, Cliff Edwards ('Ukulele Ike' - see pages 20-1) would all take the ukulele to places that would never have seemed possible just a few years before, going on to sell millions of records in the process. It seems all you needed in those days was a good nickname.

THE DARK SIDE OF THE UKULELE

The public was thrilled to hear about the dark side of the ukulele, too. In 1929, a man called Frederick Galloway was dubbed 'The Ukulele Slayer' when he murdered Andrew Pashuta, a friend he'd made through playing the instrument. They had a drunken argument that turned nasty. Galloway killed Pashuta and then had the gall to steal the dead man's ukulele. The police only tracked him down after he pawned the uke, proving that retribution is sure to follow should you steal another man's ukulele (or kill them, for that matter). He was to serve life in Folsom Prison.

This shady aspect to the uke also made an appearance in the UK. In Agatha Christie's 1930 short story *The Bird With the Broken Wing*, Mr Satterthwaite challenges the suspected murderer: 'Mabelle came back into this room for her ukelele [sic]. You had taken the string off as you fiddled with it just before. You caught her round the throat with it and strangled her... And you put another string on the ukelele - *but it was the wrong string*, that's why you were stupid.' An elementary ukulele murderer's mistake, I think you'll agree.

WORLD DOMINATION?

Like any craze (or a nasty virus), the popularity of the ukulele was bound to spread, and before long ukes were on the march into Australia, Japan, New Zealand and Great Britain. One notable beneficiary of the instrument's popularity was George Formby, the cheery Lancastrian banjo-ukulele strummer who became the best-known and highest-paid star in Britain during the 1930s and 1940s.

This modest four-stringed instrument had travelled from Portugal to Madeira to Hawaii, across America, and was now advancing back across Europe. Resistance was futile. For the time being, at least, the ukulele had well and truly conquered the world.

But all good things must come to an end, and this saturation of ukuleles could only lead to a wave of public antipathy towards our plucky little friend. During the Jazz Age of the 1920s, ukuleles were everywhere and must have been impossible to hide from. I have sympathy for those not afflicted by the ukulele bug (and for some of those who were), because you can have Too Much of a Good Thing (although I speak as one who got married to the sound of 150 kazoos tooting 'Here Comes the Bride').

The 1930s were the time of the Great Depression, following the Wall Street Crash of 1929, and one thing we all know is that when you're feeling depressed, the sound of your neighbour strumming cheerily on his ukulele can have one of two effects: it can either

1900s

temporarily cheer you up, or it can make you leap over the garden wall, grab the ukulele and use it as a trampoline. This latter option seems to have been the popular choice of the time.

While the British were thrilling to the sound of George Formby strumming his banjo-

1879: Machete arrives in Hawaii

Madeira (Machete) 15th century

Cavaquinho (Portugal)

1900s

1900s

1900s

1920s

2000s

2000s

2000s

2000s

N
E
S
U

ukulele, sales of ukes in America during the 1930s plummeted. People had less time and money for frivolous indulgences and, besides, music was becoming more freely accessible via radio and jukeboxes. People stored their ukes in their attics and got on with the serious business of trying to

earn a crust. With the Second World War also on the horizon, it was going to take something special to turn the ukulele's fortunes around.

Above: From Africa/Arabia (1) to Portugal (2), Madeira (3) and on to Hawaii (4): the bug has spread across the globe.

THE SECOND WORLD WAR TURNS THE UKULELE INTO A KIDS' TOY

Bizarrely, it was a Second World War innovation that would prove to be the catalyst for the rebirth of the ukulele, but this time in the form of a children's toy. During the war, the American Government pumped heaps of cash into the development of new plastic materials that could be used in manufacturing because of the scarcity of resources at the time. Thermoplastics could be moulded into any shape you wanted and were amazingly robust; they were used in all sorts of wartime manufacturing, from aircraft parts to cutlery.

After the war, this technology was made available to all, and the first company to see the potential of plastic to produce a cheap ukulele was toy manufacturer Mattel. Their moulded-plastic Uke-a-Doodle (whoever thought of that

name needs a good talking to) was marketed directly at children and was massively popular - if a little, well, on the crap side. Mattel sold many millions of Uke-a-Doodles over the next ten years (probably making up a good chunk of the plastic waste miserably floating around our modern-day oceans).

The first proper instrument maker to seize on the remarkable toughness and mouldability of plastic was Italian-born Mario Maccaferri. In Europe he'd been the brains behind Django Reinhardt's favourite guitar, but it would be in America that he'd enjoy his greatest financial success as the manufacturer of what's widely regarded as the greatest plastic ukulele, the Maccaferri Islander. It was very cleverly built from a space-age-sounding plastic called

Opposite: The elegantly attired Mario Maccaferri demonstrates the waterproof nature of his plastic ukulele by making it swim with the fishes. Interestingly, ukuleles also make good homes for hamsters.

Right: With a Chord Master you could play any of six chords at the touch of a button. Good news for the sausage-fingered plucker.

Far Right: The 'overall Hawaiian decor' was about the best thing you could say about a Uke-a-Doodle.

UKE-A-DOODLE

OVERALL HAWAIIAN DECOR

COMPLETE WITH PICK

BRILLIANT NEW COLORS

Photos : Antoine Carolus

Styron and, unlike the Uke-a-Doodle, had a feel and intonation that could compete with many handmade wooden ukuleles.

After teaming up with the biggest television personality of late-1940s and 1950s America - the Brylcreemed, ukulele-playing Arthur Godfrey - Maccaferri began production of his new Styron ukulele. Godfrey was a supremely gifted on-air salesman and, once the influential presenter plugged the Islander on his TV show, sales rocketed - Maccaferri would sell 350,000 ukuleles in 1950 alone. Mario's daughter, Eliane, tells me that she worked in their Bronx factory in the 1950s, testing the ukuleles. 'I'd hit them on the conveyor belt to see if they sounded right and didn't have any cracks. The next person would tuck in the pick, the next would

bag it up, and so on. That evening I remember my mum said, "That's it, we just packed 10,000 ukuleles today!"'

Cheaper to produce and cheaper to buy (the cheapest model, the Ukette, was only $2.98, including a how-to book), but still very playable, Maccaferri's plastic ukes were always going to be the popular choice for parents looking for an affordable starter instrument for their children. He went on to produce many more, from the baritone to the visual Chord Master, a bizarre device that fitted onto the neck of the ukulele and allowed you to play different chords at the touch of a button. Many other manufacturers followed suit, and even Elvis jumped on the bandwagon with his very own plastic ukulele.

THE UKE OUT IN THE COLD

Although no one knew it at the time, the children who were born in the 1940s and 1950s and played these cheap instruments would grow up to be the rock 'n' roll stars of the 1960s and 1970s. Out-and-out rockers like Jimi Hendrix (see page 70-1), Eric Clapton and Neil Young (see page 65) all got their first taste of music playing ukuleles like Maccaferri's.

The ukulele's journey through the 1960s and 1970s was never going to be easy, though. Competing with an amplified rock 'n' roll revolution was nigh on impossible, and the uke went into a mini-hibernation over this period. Pretty much anything called a ukulele was seen as out of date, although a few anomalous ukuleles made it through the net. The Beatles promoted a 'guitar' that was really a four-string ukulele.

In Hawaii things also died down and, although jazz ukulelist Lyle Ritz and Hawaiians Eddie Kamae and Herb Ohta were popular, it seemed that the heyday of the ukulele had passed.

There were, though, a few people who simply would not let the ukulele rest. In America, Tiny Tim and Ian Whitcomb (as well as astronaut Neil Armstrong) strummed on.

Ian Whitcomb had scored a Top Ten rock 'n' roll hit, 'You Turn Me On', in the USA in 1965 and went on to tour with some of the biggest bands of the era, but the purchase of his Martin ukulele, and his subsequent use of it in his recordings, 'marked the end of my rock 'n' roll career', so little did the public think of the uke at that time.

Meanwhile in Canada, another important figure was going against the grain of popular taste. J Chalmers Doane, who headed the music curriculum for all Halifax schools, put the ukulele at the centre of music teaching, getting thousands of children started on the uke throughout the 1960s and 1970s, including modern virtuoso James Hill (see page 36). He preached ukulele with a missionary zeal, as can be heard on the fantastically positive *Ukulele Yes!* album he produced.

Below: J Chalmers Doane's 1972 album was performed by The Ukuleles of Halifax, consisting of 35 ukuleles and a double bass. Their difficult second album 'Ukuleles on Tour' followed in 1973.

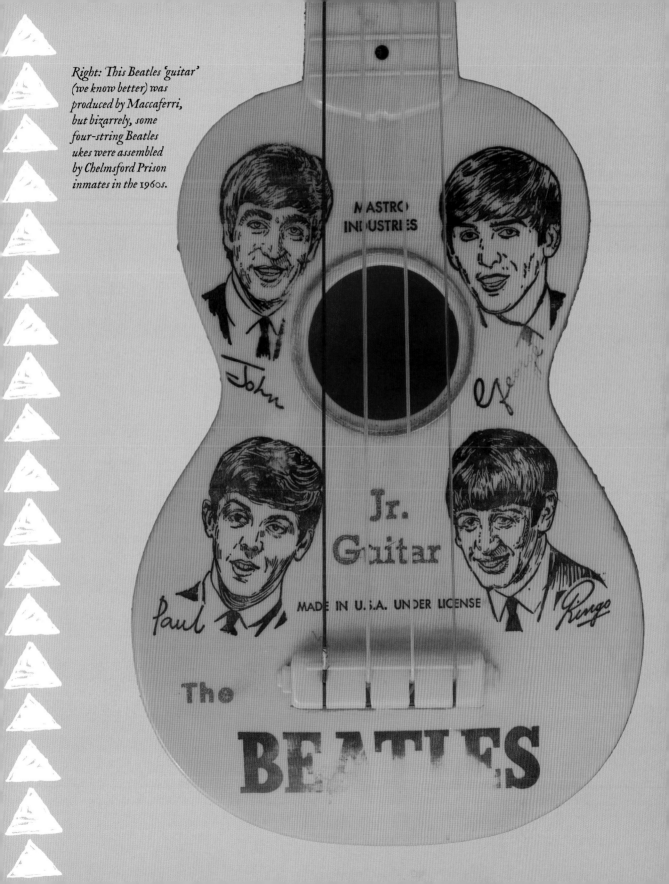

Right: This Beatles 'guitar' (we know better) was produced by Maccaferri, but bizarrely, some four-string Beatles ukes were assembled by Chelmsford Prison inmates in the 1960s.

UKULELE REVIVAL

Since the mid-1980s, the ukulele has seen a gradual revival, to the point where now people even want to buy books about it (as you, or someone whose name you're currently cursing, have done). There were always a few people who never stopped promoting the instrument, but recently, and especially since the birth of the internet, the ukulele seems to be well and truly here to stay.

The best place to start with the modern-day revival of the ukulele, in Europe at least, is in 1985 with the birth of the Ukulele Orchestra of Great Britain. The UOGB heralded the beginnings of a fresh perspective on the ukulele, one that hadn't been seen since the 1920s - that it could be cool. Playing material that would previously have seemed unthinkable on a uke - from songs by Otis Redding to classical pieces by Tchaikovsky - the UOGB were pushing the boundaries of what was deemed to be the instrument's 'acceptable' repertoire. While the rest of Britain looked on in wide-eyed astonishment, the Orchestra steadily built up a large and loyal following, and were quickly pursued by TV and record companies.

While the Ukulele Orchestra were steadily plucking their way around Britain, Americans began to get in on the act. Seven years later,

in 1992, Jim Beloff would discover an old ukulele at the Pasadena Rose Bowl Flea Market, which would spur him to create his Flea Market Music website, produce his own newfangled triangular 'Fluke' ukulele and publish countless how-to guides and strum-along books. His indefatigable enthusiasm for the instrument helped reinvigorate the ukulele scene in America, including now-dormant websites like Midnight Ukulele Disco, which broadcast weird and wonderful ukulele cabaret from New York in the late 1990s and early 2000s.

In Hawaii, too, the ukulele found a new icon in the colossal shape of Israel Kamakawiwo'ole, a velvet-voiced ukulele player whose 1993 album *Facing Futures* defied many people's expectations to become the first Hawaiian album ever to go platinum. For many young people, Israel's songs were the first serious ukulele playing they'd ever heard, and his influence within and beyond Hawaii was enormous. And where Hawaiian music goes, Japan is always sure to follow - ukulele sales boomed in Japan during this period, and continue to do so. When the Ukulele Orchestra of Great Britain toured Japan in 1994 they were amazed to find a thriving ukulele scene there, though with a mostly Hawaiian bent.

As the 2000s have progressed, the ukulele seems to have taken an even stronger hold on popular culture. It's become the go-to instrument for use in television advert soundtracks, adding instant charm and down-to-earth wholesomeness to the image of even the most hard-nosed multinational corporations. Not only that, but just like in the 1920s, celebrities seem to be flocking to the uke as well. Actors such as Johnny Depp, Gary Oldman and Pierce Brosnan are all very open

Where the uke goes, celebrity follows. These days more and more pop and rock stars, such as Taylor Swift (top) and Paul McCartney (above) are playing the uke without laughing.

about their ukulele fascinations. These days there's no shame in playing the uke; quite the opposite, in fact - it can make careers. Even politicians aren't immune to the charms of the uke: ex British prime minister Tony Blair was recently spotted plucking a baritone uke on holiday, presumably hoping that some of its popularity might rub off on him.

In Britain, a few key moments pushed the ukulele into the wider musical world, like when Joe Brown and Paul McCartney plucked their ukuleles at the memorial concert for George Harrison at the Royal Albert Hall in 2002, and when the Ukulele Orchestra of Great Britain were invited to play at the BBC Proms, that venerated British institution of classical music, in 2008. Their performance (to a full house of over 6,000 people - the fastest-selling late-night Prom in history) represented something of a high point for the ukulele, the UOGB and the popularity of the instrument.

Spurred on by popular acceptance of the instrument, plenty of mainstream musicians are jumping on the bandwagon. Taylor Swift, Amanda Palmer, Eddie Vedder and Elvis Costello are just some of those who have used ukuleles completely unironically in their live shows and recorded work. They can play them in public with absolutely no fear of audiences turning up their noses. How far we have come!

Across the world we've also been swamped by a tidal wave of ukulele festivals, ukulele workshops and even ukulele-only shops, such as the Duke of Uke in London. Meanwhile, in countries from New Zealand to America to Germany, ukulele orchestras have popped up, inspired by the example of the Ukulele Orchestra of Great Britain.

It can sometimes seem as though everyone has a ukulele these days. Musician and ukulele revivalist Ian Whitcomb sees the ukulele as a democratic and social instrument: 'I'm glad the revival is happening - it's like the modern-day equivalent of skiffle; anyone can do it. I keep meeting new players, and these days it can be more like playing musical bingo. It's a social thing, like a Billy Butlin holiday camp.'

Despite this, I firmly believe that the ukulele is still, and will remain, an outsider instrument. Uncategorizable, unconventional and often untunable, it will always provoke both wonder and ridicule, and rightly so. It's one of the only instruments out there that keeps music truly playful, and in the right hands it can be a thing not just of great comedy, but also of great beauty. There aren't many instruments like a ukulele.

WHAT NEXT FOR THE UKE?

So, where will it all end? If nothing else, the ukulele has proved itself to be a survivor - the ultimate bounce-back instrument. History has taught us that when popular culture declares the little plucker to be dead and buried, it never is. It's only hibernating.

Not only is the ukulele being embraced by modern composers and musicians, it's also making serious headway by infiltrating school music curriculums around the world, creating a whole new generation of ukulele players. More and more music teachers are dispensing with violins and recorders, preferring instead to use the ukulele to get children started in music. Cheap, friendly and often colourfully decorated as well, the ukulele offers teachers a simple and effective way to help kids understand how music is constructed.

With recent advances in technology, computer programmers have been plotting ways to suck the ukulele into smartphones and tablets. These days there are touchscreen ukuleles available (check out the horrifying Futulele), and even 3D printed ukuleles have begun rolling off the presses. Pretty soon you should be able to design and print your own uke from the comfort of your own home. All you'll need is a robot to play it for you.

People are also finding that the ukulele has unexpected psychological benefits. Businessmen these days are using it as a stress-busting tool, with strumming and singing workshops regularly laid on for overworked executives. In Israel, the ukulele is even doing its bit to build bridges between divided communities. Ukuleles for Peace is an organization run by Israel resident Paul Moore that unites Israeli and Palestinian children by getting them to play ukulele and sing together.

I think one of the main reasons the ukulele is going to become ever more popular in Western culture is that it offers us the all-too-rare chance to sing together. When was the last time you wandered into your local pub and stumbled across an impromptu sing-along? Not for a while, I'll wager. And as the number of people going to church on Sunday to holler some hymns dwindles, it seems there are fewer and fewer public spaces where people can sing together.

The ukulele offers people an alternative, non-hierarchical path into music. In a world where music has become something you only listen to on your own through headphones, people are showing

that they still have a basic desire to get together and make a racket. They don't need amplifiers, drum kits or keyboards to do it - the humble uke is enough. Ukulele groups for youngsters as well as the elderly are booming. Add to that the push the instrument is getting from schools, and there can be only one destiny for the ukulele - world domination.

Like a clever rat in a nuclear holocaust, the ukulele always seems able to reinvent itself and live another day.

Below: The wonderful Ukuleles for Peace brings fractured communities together by using the humble ukulele to unite Israeli and Palestinian families and young people.

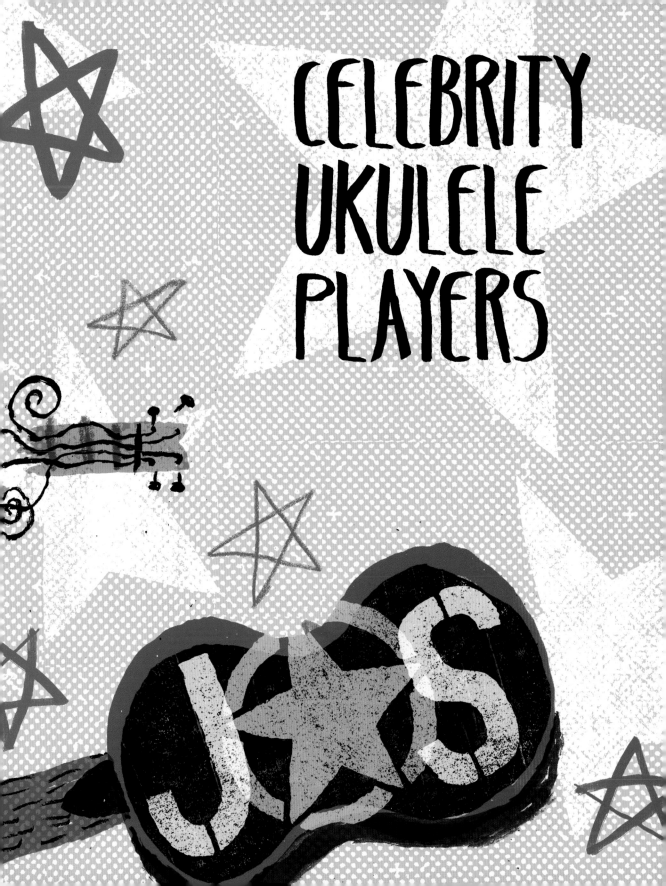

UNLIKELY UKULELE PLAYERS

★ ★ ★ ★ ★ ★ ★ ★ ★ ★ ★ ★ ★ ★

A whole book could be written about the famous musicians who owe a debt to the humble ukulele. For nearly all these people, the ukulele was the spark that lit their interest in playing a musical instrument. Syd Barrett, Jimi Hendrix, David Bowie, José Feliciano and many more all started on the ukulele.

ELVIS PRESLEY 1935-1977

Yep, Elvis played a ukulele. He also recorded a ukulele album. Even more than that, he based his iconic dancing style on that of loose-limbed bluesman Charlie Burse, the 'Ukulele Kid'. He was, in truth, nothing but a uke dog.

While it's by no means a masterpiece, the soundtrack to the 1961 American musical romantic comedy *Blue Hawaii* is saturated with strumming (a whopping seven ukulele players joined in the recording sessions). Elvis even sings the Hawaiian classic 'Aloha 'Oe,' which kicks off with a frenzied ukulele crescendo. He squeezes in a ton of other Hawaiian-esque tunes, from the questionable 'Rock-a-Hula Baby' to the more soothing 'Hawaiian Sunset'. The movie did feature one classic Presley tune, though - 'Can't Help Falling in Love' - and the public delighted in Elvis's ukulele strumming throughout the hit movie.

The King also bears some responsibility for the spread of ukuleles across the USA, with Elvis-branded plastic ukuleles popping up in music shops everywhere. Elvis himself owned a very nice Martin ukulele, which just recently came up for auction (guide price $60,000-$80,000, gadzooks).

But the King owes the ukulele much more than just a bit part in *Blue Hawaii*. When he was still in high school, Elvis would visit Beale Street in Memphis to watch the black musicians who played there. In *Beale, Black and Blue*, a history of Beale Street, the young Presley is described 'watching old Charlie Burse, "Ukulele Ike [sic]", twitching his knee, rocking his pelvis and rolling his syllables during a show...at a Beale Street honky-tonk (the style Elvis copied to launch the blue-suede blues).' Music promoter Robert Henry remembers taking Elvis to watch Burse play: 'He would watch the coloured singers...and then he got to doing it the same way as them. He got that shaking, that wiggle, from Charlie Burse...right there at the Gray Mule on Beale.'

So, strange as it may seem, one of Elvis's key influences was a ukulele player. You can read about Charlie Burse ('Ukulele Kid'), the man who can be credited with giving us Elvis's iconic dance moves, on page 34.

During the 'Blue Hawaii' recording sessions it was a Hawaiian, Bernie Kaai Lewis, who taught Elvis how to play ukulele. Elvis loved Hawaii – it became his favourite holiday destination and he even had the 'Jungle Room' at Graceland decked out in eccentric Polynesian style.

JONI MITCHELL 1943-

Joni Mitchell has always been one of my favourite songwriters, so it was with great delight that I found out she'd started on the ukulele. She'd wanted a guitar, but her mother had objected because of its 'hillbilly' associations (quite right, too). So in 1957 she took the ukulele path: 'I went out and bought myself a ukulele...and I plunked my way through most of the summer.'

It was a $36 baritone ukulele, and on it she'd pluck Kingston Trio songs and other folk tunes learned from a Pete Seeger record. She made her first ever appearance on Canadian TV accompanied by her ukulele in 1961, after being spotted singing at a local wiener roast. Her auspicious debut replaced a cancelled moose-hunting programme. 'So I played my six-song repertoire with a baritone ukulele on my own half-hour TV special. People recognized me on the street next day. So I was bitten by the bug.'

It was an unpromising start, but Mitchell would hit the big time once she began playing guitar (and also the four-stringed dulcimer).

NEIL YOUNG 1945-

It's said that Neil Young got into music after seeing Elvis on *The Ed Sullivan Show*, but I like to think that it was his father who was the real inspiration. In an interview Neil recalled: 'Well, my father played a little ukulele. It just happened. I felt it. I couldn't stop thinking about it.'

He was given a plastic ukulele by his parents and quickly began to work out tunes on it. 'He would close the door of his room at the top of the stairs,' Scott (his father) said, 'and we would hear *plunk*, pause while he moved again, *plunk*.' Neil played uke for several years, but finally got saddled with a guitar, poor thing.

PETE TOWNSHEND 1945-

The Who's legendary songwriter has had more brushes with the ukulele than hot dinners. Although he famously used a uke to great effect on 'Blue, Red and Grey,' his relationship with the instrument goes right back to his childhood.

On a holiday to the Isle of Man in the mid-1950s, he and a mischievous friend sneaked backstage at a George Formby show and pulled the curtain down on the Lancastrian mid-way through a performance. 'It was boyish disdain, he irritated us because he appeared so happy, plunking away on his little banjo-ukulele.'

In 1968, while working as an A&R man, Pete attended one of Tiny Tim's first gigs in New York. An instant convert, he almost signed Tiny to Track Records, only to be outbid by a bigger US label. Pete admired Tiny as the unique musicologist he was, and even considered casting him for the song 'Pinball Wizard': 'I imagined it would sound really great on 100 ukuleles.'

He bought a Martin ukulele in 1971 and went on to use ukes as composing tools, favouring the eccentric ukulele 're-entrant' tuning (see page 98): 'I still use ukuleles to compose on. If you fingerpick it, the high note creates all sorts of unexpected sparkling arpeggios'.

These days, he's never far from a ukulele: 'You can keep one in the bathroom and instead of reading a book you just pull out the ukulele and have a plonk away.' However, it's not always a straightforward relationship: 'I have a love-hate thing with the ukulele. It's a rather low-grade instrument...I just hate the 'plunk' of it - there's just no sustain in those nylon strings.'

But it has to be said that they're much less costly to smash up at the end of a gig.

Opposite: Joni Mitchell, Canada's answer to George Formby.

WARREN BUFFETT 1930-

Billionaire business mogul and economics guru Warren Buffett is one of the richest people in the world. Despite his vast wealth, he has a reputation for being unostentatious and cautious with his money, and it's rumoured that he plans to leave 99 per cent of his wealth to good causes after his death. Of course, like most good eggs, he's a ukulele player.

He learned to play the ukulele in college to impress a girl he was keen on, but, he says, 'It didn't work.' (A rare bad gamble for Mr Buffett, one imagines.) These days he's rarely seen without his ukulele, playing it at his investment firm's annual bash, and even more recently on state television in China (where he's something of a hero), giving a charming version of 'I've Been Working on the Railroad' to celebrate the Chinese New Year. It's a wonderful clip, which you can see on YouTube, but I think it's out-weirded by a ukulele duet he performed with Jon Bon Jovi. Yep, Jon Bon Jovi.

Above: Buffet performs 'Red River Valley' to the Berkshire Hathaway shareholders with the Quebe Sisters in 2008.

Above: The whereabouts of Armstrong's MQF ukulele remain a mystery. His wife Carol and son Rick claim no knowledge of it. Conspiracy theory, anyone?

NEIL ARMSTRONG 1930-2012

Although you might not think it probable, the ukulele has a rich history in the hands of astronauts. Without doubt, the ukulele's greatest brush with a spaceman was when Neil Armstrong played one straight after becoming the first man to walk on the moon. When he, Buzz Aldrin and Michael Collins returned to earth after their epic journey in 1969, they had to spend 65 hours in a Mobile Quarantine

Facility (MQF) so that scientists could be sure they hadn't picked up any 'moon germs' on their mission. The MQF was a specially converted Airstream trailer stationed aboard the *USS Hornet*. Late on the night of 24 July 1969, Don Blair, a radio reporter, happened to be in the right place at the right time and took this incredible shot of Neil Armstrong through one of the windows, having a strum on his uke to pass the time.

Locked in a tight spot for 65 hours with a man armed with just a ukulele might not be everyone's idea of a good time, but I have been reliably informed by John Hirasaki (who, at his own risk, was the only technician inside the MQF with the astronauts) that the experience wasn't all bad.

'Neil would bring it out and strum on it a bit. He could play well. It lightened things up after what had been an extremely stressful mission.' It seems that the ukulele was a welcome addition inside the MQF after all. 'The atmosphere among them was electric', John says. 'They were all very excited, you could hear it just from the tones of their voices. Just imagine if you and your friends went on an adventure that no one else had ever been on! So the ukulele helped to relax him. You're in a pressure cooker all this time and it was nice to be able to wind down a bit - the ukulele enabled us all to do that.'

The song Neil was playing in the picture remains a mystery, sadly. Don Blair has thought long and hard about it. He told me, 'I only hope it was "Fly Me to the Moon".' My vote's for Sun Ra's 'Space is the Place'.

UKES IN SPACE

As well as Neil Armstrong, there are a surprising number of other ukulele-wielding astronauts.

A little-known cosmic strummer is John W Young, commander of the Apollo 16 mission and the ninth man to walk on the moon. He was also a keen ukulele player who'd entertain the team with his strumming and harmonica playing at NASA parties. Even today, a ukulele is kept aboard the International Space Station for the use of the crews. US astronaut Kevin Ford has played the instrument on board while orbiting 400km (249 miles) above the earth.

The ukulele is clearly not just aiming for world domination; it has its sights set on the entire universe.

Below: If there is life on other planets, do they, like us, carry ukuleles aboard their spacecraft? Kevin Ford strums a thoughtful C chord aboard the ISS.

PAUL McCARTNEY 1942–
JOHN LENNON 1940–1980

Back in 2000, Paul McCartney told the *Daily Express*, 'John really loved his mother, idol-worshipped her…She played the ukulele and to this day, if I ever meet grown-ups who play ukuleles, I love them.'

Both John Lennon and Paul McCartney had ukulele connections. John's mother and Paul's father and cousin all played the ukulele and so, spurred on by George Harrison's enthusiasm for the instrument, ukuleles were never far from the Fab Four, and they would often break into George Formby jams (as they did during the *Let It Be* sessions).

On tour the year after George Harrison's death in 2001, Paul performed a beautifully stripped-down version of 'Something' on a Gibson ukulele given to him by George. He reminisced to the crowd about how 'when you went round to George's house, after you'd had dinner, the ukuleles would come out'. A good digestive aid, no doubt.

GEORGE HARRISON 1943–2001

One of the most famous rock 'n' roll artists to be an out-and-out ukulele nut was George Harrison. This was a man who absolutely loved the ukulele and was never without one.

In 1966, when The Beatles were beginning their fascination with Hare Krishna, George and John Lennon took a trip to Greece, sailing in the Aegean Sea. In his book, *Working Class Mystic*, Gary Tillery writes, 'George and John stood on the deck of their ship for hours with ukulele-banjos, chanting the maha-mantra to the sky and wind and sea.' It must have been quite a sight.

A member of the George Formby Society, as well as the Ukulele Society of Great Britain, Harrison was something of a ukulele evangelist and gave them away at every opportunity.

Tom Petty recalls a visit from George in the 1990s. He arrived with two ukuleles - one for Petty - and proceeded to teach him how to play. They spent a jolly afternoon plunking away together and, as George left (after explaining to Petty that the ukulele was 'a machine that kills sadness'), he opened the boot of his car to reveal a pile of ukes and gave him three more. Petty explains: 'He really got into the ukulele…it gave him so much joy, you know…The rest of his life was ukulele. He played the hell out of the thing.'

Right up until the end of his life, George played the ukulele. His friend Tony Bramwell reminisced about George's strumming sessions, 'I'll never forget about the ukulele jams he had with Joe Brown and Gary Moore in his local pub, The Crooked Billet in Henley. Deep Purple's Jon Lord would often join in on piano.' An all-star ukulele cast, if there ever was one.

Opposite: John Lennon backstage at the Finsbury Park Astoria in 1963. Left: George Harrison in a rare photo without his ukulele.

JIMI HENDRIX 1942-1970

In *Jimi Hendrix: A Brother's Story*, Leon Hendrix recalls that, for Jimi, 'The ukulele was like a key that opened the door to another world. The search for complete expression began, and he was going to follow the path as far as it was going to take him.'

Jimi Hendrix is perhaps one of the most surprising members of our ukulele-playing panoply. Born to a poor family in Seattle in 1942, he was obsessed with music from an early age. In his desperation for an instrument, Jimi took to building imaginary guitars from broomsticks, which he insisted on taking into school, but it was a chance encounter with a dusty old ukulele that would be Jimi's entry into the world of music.

His brother, Leon, remembers the moment when Jimi first laid eyes on the uke. He and Jimi (known to the family as Buster) were helping their father clear out an old garage in Seattle. While their father took a break in a nearby pub, 'Buster and I kept digging through the garage', says Leon, 'looking for the next piece of buried treasure. Before long, Buster walked out holding a beat-up ukulele. When he plucked at it a few times, a smile swept across his face.'

Back at home, Jimi played with the old ukulele (which only had one string) for hours and hours: 'Even though he was playing single notes, he still followed along to Elvis Presley songs on the radio. Buster did it all by ear and matched up the notes.' At the sight of this, his father searched high and low and eventually managed to get hold of an acoustic guitar for his son. Jimi would never look back, and went on to become the king of the electric guitar.

Opposite: Where ukuleles tread, guitar stardom is quick to follow. Although no known photos exist of Jimi with his uke, this picture shows what he must have looked like wielding his axe (or hatchet).

HENDRIX AND TINY TIM

Rock journalist Keith Altham tells me that when he accompanied Jimi Hendrix on a plane to the Monterey International Pop Festival in 1967, a hook-nosed man with long, greasy black hair stood up mid-flight, armed with a ukulele, and launched into 'Tiptoe Through the Tulips'. It was, of course, Tiny Tim (see pages 22-3), also on his way to the festival. Jimi was reduced to hysterics, doubled up in his chair, weeping with laughter at this unexpected mid-air performance. Bizarre though it must have been, I like to think that, briefly at least, Jimi remembered how the ukulele had got him started on his amazing musical journey. The moment created an unlikely kinship between two very different performers, Tiny and Jimi, united at 30,000ft by the little jumping flea.

DICK DALE 1937–

Dick Dale is known as 'The King of Surf Guitar'. His version of the Middle Eastern folk tune 'Misirlou' was a worldwide hit in 1962 (and more recently featured in the Quentin Tarantino movie *Pulp Fiction*), and his trademark heavy guitar sound was a fundamental influence on the young ears of both Jimi Hendrix and Eddie Van Halen. But Dick Dale would never have got anywhere without his ukulele.

Born in Boston to Polish and Lebanese parents, Dale had always fantasized about being a guitar-strumming cowboy like Hank Williams. So he collected enough Coke bottles to earn six dollars, and walked seven miles to a music store to buy a plastic ukulele. Now that's dedication. He explained: 'I bought a chord book and tried to put my fingers where the book told me. It was nearly impossible. I used to tape my fingers into a chord on the neck of the uke before I went to sleep, hoping that a fairy godmother would come along and tap my fingers and I would wake up with my fingers staying there.'

Once he'd got the hang of it, he wanted to move on to the guitar and asked some local hobos for advice. One of them told him the secret: 'Well, kid, just pretend you're still playing the uke. Play the four strings and muffle the others. No one's gonna know. Basically, I saw the guitar as an exploded version of the uke...I played the guitar this way until I got to California.'

Right: Although Dick Dale finally managed to master the guitar, he still had to be reminded to face to the audience at gigs.

QUEEN'S BRIAN MAY 1947–
ROGER TAYLOR 1949–

The stargazing 1970s guitar hero Brian May still has his dad's 'George Formby' banjo-ukulele, which his father carried with him throughout the Second World War. Brian says that the ukulele 'is how I learned to play the guitar. The chord shapes that my dad taught me transferred quite easily onto the guitar, and I remember I got a guitar for my seventh birthday and started working out the chords.'

Years later, Brian would use a surreal burst of Formby-style ukulele in 'Bring Back That Leroy Brown' on the Queen album *Sheer Heart Attack*, as well as plunking away throughout 'Good Company' on *A Night at the Opera*.

Queen's drummer, Roger Taylor, was also a sucker for a ukulele. He got the bug when he was eight, playing ukulele in a skiffle group called The Bubbling Over Boys. Two guitars, a tea-chest bass and Roger on ukulele. They only ever performed one gig, at a school dance, but his ukulele strumming with them was to be his first, powerful taste of the crazily hedonistic lifestyle of a heavy rock group. Or perhaps not.

Brian May breaks into a strum on his father's banjo-ukulele at a Queen concert in New York City in 1977.

DAVID BYRNE 1952–

As an artist who's always gone his own way, it's comforting to know that David Byrne made room for the ukulele in his repertoire. It really is the perfect instrument for him, being so infectiously rhythmic. After writing his first song – the wonderfully titled 'Bald-Headed Woman' – when he was 15, Byrne began performing Chuck Berry and Eddie Cochran tunes on the ukulele at high-school shows.

Years later, at art school, he'd pick up the ukulele again when he formed a duo called Bizadi with accordion-playing friend Mark Kehoe. They travelled around the country, busking standards like 'Pennies From Heaven' and 'The Glory of Love,' as well as more modern stuff, such as '96 Tears' by Question Mark & the Mysterians. In his book *How Music Works*, David says that playing outside with a ukulele forced him to perform more and to strike crazy poses in the street. We'd see more crazy poses from Mr Byrne later in his career, but it's nice to know where they began.

Talking Heads biographer David Bowman believes that the ukulele defines Byrne. Byrne told him: 'I've always liked the idea of a portable music-making device, a take-anywhere, always ready instrument.' Dancer Twyla Tharp, Byrne's girlfriend in the early 1980s, agreed. She believed the great tension in the tiny instrument was well suited to her lover's energy: '…his normal rhythm was quadruple time and the ukulele worked well in that small, bright range.'

So if the ukulele was a person, it might well be David Byrne (although I'm not sure Hawaii's Queen Lili'uokalani would agree).

Left: In an effort to keep his four-string habit quiet, David Byrne would often hide his ukulele behind his back.

GEORGE BENSON 1943-

Another guitar master to begin life on the humble ukulele is ten-time Grammy Award-winner George Benson. One of six children born to a very poor family in Pittsburgh, he started playing ukulele aged just six, having been taught by his stepfather, Thomas Collier. George says he used the ukulele to woo the girls at school. (The ukulele is well known for its powers of attraction. Isn't it? Hello? Anyone there?) At seven years old he was sitting in at gigs with his stepfather, singing, dancing and playing the ukulele.

George eventually grew big enough to get his hands around a full-size guitar neck, but the ukulele would always remain a special instrument for him. He told me, 'It was a great starter instrument that prepared me for the guitar, but I wish I'd continued to study the uke'. In 2013, he went so far as to include a fantastic early recording of his younger self, 'Lil' Georgie Benson', singing Nat King Cole's version of 'Mona Lisa' on the album *Inspiration: A Tribute to Nat King Cole*. On it, the eight-year-old George charmingly accompanies himself on a wonky old ukulele.

'I used to think the ukulele was a novelty instrument, but my experience listening to other uke players in Hawaii changed my mind. It is a bonafide, beautiful-sounding musical instrument.' Quite right, George.

A seven-year-old George Benson performs with his step-father Tom Collier at the Little Paris Nightclub in Pittsburgh.

JOE STRUMMER 1952-2002

In 1970, The Clash front man Joe Strummer met musician (and ukulele owner) Tymon Dogg, while studying at the Central School of Art and Design in London. On Dogg's busking missions around London, Joe would accompany him, collecting the money, and this clearly inspired the young man. Helen Cherry, an art-school friend, recalls some of Joe's first attempts at songwriting: 'I remember Joe singing this chorus, "I'm gonna be sick / I wanna puke up in a bucket of water," and trying to play it on Tymon's ukulele.' Not exactly 'London Calling,' but you've got to start somewhere, I suppose.

He finally bit the bullet and decided to buy a ukulele of his own. 'I bought a ukulele, 'cos I figured that had to be easier than a guitar, having only four strings.' He paid £2.99 for it and learned some Chuck Berry songs to busk on the Underground. It was on one such excursion that Joe had something of an epiphany: 'I was playing "Sweet Little Sixteen" on the ukulele and an American happened to walk past and he stopped in front of me and went, "I don't believe it, I can't believe it," and he began smacking his forehead, and staggering around, and nearly fainting, and I stopped playing and said, "What? What?" And he went, "You're playing Chuck Berry on a ukulele!" And I hadn't considered it to be odd at all. I only started to think it was a bit odd after this American...was nearly banging his head on the subway wall with the ridiculousness of it...Eventually I got a guitar.'

Left: Strummer strumming outside JFK Stadium, Philadelphia in 1982. Even when he was in The Clash he never forgot his ukulele ways.

EDDIE VEDDER 1964–

After 20 years fronting Pearl Jam, one of America's noisiest grunge bands, singer Eddie Vedder surprised everyone by suddenly recording an album of ukulele-only songs. He called it, well, *Ukulele Songs*, and on it he plays 'sad songs on a happy instrument'.

Eddie's relationship with the ukulele has been quietly constant throughout his life. His mother bought him a beaten-up uke at a yard sale when he was a child and, more recently, he bought one on impulse while surfing in Hawaii. He relates, 'As far as inanimate objects being friends goes, I think that's right on the list. My Martin ukulele is a work of art. It's going to live long after me.' Lord help us if he buys a set of bagpipes on a whim when he's next in Scotland.

But it was when he heard Pete Townshend's 'Blue, Red and Grey' as a 13-year-old kid that he first took the ukulele seriously. 'That made it feel like, no question, it was a legitimate instrument and you could write music on it.' The two have gone on to become great pals, united by their love of the diminutive guitar.

Eddie says, 'This little four-string songwriting tool started changing the way I brought songs to the group.' I can just imagine the enthusiasm he felt when he first brought his ukulele along to a Pearl Jam rehearsal. One only hopes that his grunge-mates felt the same.

Above: Vedder would sometimes sit poised for hours, unable to decide which chord to pluck next…

DAVID BOWIE 1947–

David Bowie's dad, John Jones, had always hoped his son might become an entertainer and, by way of encouragement, he bought young David a ukulele. What a sensible gift it turned out to be. Bowie eagerly set about learning some chords.

While enrolling for the Cub Scouts in Bromley, UK, the nine-year-old David met George Underwood. A shared love of music and a thirst for adventure connected the two boys, and it wasn't long before Bowie was planning their first gig together.

In the summer of 1958 they travelled to a Cub Scouts summer camp on the Isle of Wight. Now a successful artist, George Underwood still remembers it vividly: 'We were picked up in a big kind of furniture truck. It arrived at my house and when the doors opened, in the back there was David, sitting with his ukulele and a tea-chest bass he'd built out of a pole and a bit of gut.'

On the way to the campsite they wrote down all the lyrics they could remember to a couple of Lonnie Donegan songs, 'Puttin' on the Style' and 'Gamblin' Man', and around the campfire that night they were to put on their first ever public performance, singing, scratching and plunking away on the uke and tea-chest bass. 'David was very good at harmonizing and we just gelled together. The crowd was all behind us - that would have been our joint debut performing in public. They really were the golden years!'

So David Bowie's first foray into public performance was on a ukulele? At last we can understand why he called himself 'The Thin White (D)uke'...

Right: John, I'm only strumming. Even when armed with a violin, Bowie dreamt of his ukulele round the campfire.

MARILYN MONROE 1926-1962

As Sugar Kane in *Some Like It Hot*, Marilyn Monroe really is the last word in ukulele sexiness. Wiggling her way up and down a railway carriage during her rendition of 'Runnin' Wild', ukulele in hand, she created one of the defining ukulele images of the 20th century.

She was taught ukulele in preparation for the 1959 film and by all accounts was besotted with the little instrument. Indeed, it was the prospect of singing and learning to play ukulele that, more than anything, motivated her to sign the contract. Although she was never a virtuoso, she could carry a tune on the uke and continued to play it throughout her life.

The whereabouts of her legendary white ukulele is not known, but there are many out there who would give their eye teeth for a strum of it. Ukulele boffins assure me that it was an old Martin uke that had been painted white by the studio to show up better against Marilyn's black outfit. But at least it was Jack Lemmon's double bass that took the bullet.

For me, it's her perfect delivery of this classic movie line that is unforgettable. She tells Jack Lemmon (in drag, as Daphne), 'If it wasn't for you, they'd have kicked me off the train. I'd be out in the middle of nowhere, sitting on my ukulele.' Cue thousands of men thinking about Marilyn's ukulele. George Formby would've been proud of that one.

Below: After her husband Arthur Miller was acquitted by the House Committee of Un-American Activities during the McCarthy witch hunts in 1958, the LA Times *reported that Marilyn celebrated by serenading the journalists with a rather tuneless version of 'Happy Days are Here Again' on her white ukulele.*

Opposite: Marilyn with 'Sweet Sue and Her Society Syncopators' in Some Like it Hot.

Thomas, armed only with a smile and his ukulele, on his return to Southampton in 1945. He stashed the rings he's wearing in a bar of soap throughout his capture.

THOMAS BOARDMAN 1918–

For sheer bloody-minded ukulele fanaticism in the face of misery and torture, Second World War veteran Thomas Boardman has to take first prize. A Lancashire lad, Thomas taught himself ukulele as a teenager in the 1930s. Little did he know then, but it would prove to be something of a salvation for him once war broke out.

He volunteered in 1939 but was captured in 1942 by the Japanese and imprisoned in Changi and Chunkai Prisoner of War Camps. He and his comrades suffered horrific conditions, gruelling work and paltry rations, large numbers of them dying of disease and malnutrition.

Thomas decided to try and build a ukulele with which to entertain his weary comrades. Using discarded scraps of wood, metal and bits of old Red Cross boxes, it took him just over two months to build, and is a wonderful instrument, baritone sized, and eccentrically box-shaped. He'd play songs like 'When I'm Cleaning Windows' and 'Please Don't Talk About Me When I'm Gone' for his often desperately ill colleagues. And in a strange twist, these musical performances became something that even their Japanese captors looked forward to.

Now 95, Thomas still plays, and has recently joined the George Formby Society, travelling with his son, Ron, to their yearly meetings where they enjoy the mass strum-alongs.

Thomas's ukulele is on permanent display at the Imperial War Museum North in Manchester. And, proving that a ukulele rarely needs its strings changing, it still wears the same set that Thomas put on it in the prison camp in the 1940s.

BOBBY EDWARDS 1879-1948

Plenty of people like to decorate their ukuleles, but the original ukulele-botherer was musician, artist, actor, writer and eccentric, Bobby Edwards, otherwise known as 'The Troubadour of Greenwich Village'. He famously built and painted his own vividly coloured 'Ukalyptos' ukuleles - 'The Second Cousin of the Ukulele'.

Born in Buffalo, New Jersey, he made his home in the village in 1901 after graduating from Harvard. He was a bohemian, happiest among the artists, poets and radical thinkers of downtown Manhattan. His studio was a cornucopia of artistic experimentation, and people would go just to marvel at the colourful chaos within. Bobby could often be found singing his satirical songs at local coffee shops and theatres, twanging his ukes to self-penned tunes such as 'The Sultan's Wives Have Got the Hives (From Eating Anchovies and Chives)' and 'Why Be An Industrial Slave When You Can be Crazy?', a sentiment we can all raise a glass to.

Below: 'Great lurid blobs of color on a wooden box.... And Bobby Edwards in his garret 'neath the stars, creating Eukalalies...'

GREAT LURID BLOBS OF COLOR ON A WOODEN BOX
AND BOBBY EDWARDS IN HIS GARRET NEATH THE STARS
CREATING EUKALALIES
30 GREENWICH VILLAGE NEW YORK
©JESSIE TARBOX BEALS

GET PLUCKY: HOW TO PLAY THE THING

BEFORE WE GET STARTED

I've taken the view that the reason you've chosen to play the ukulele is because you don't particularly want to have to learn how to read musical notation. If you'd wanted to do that, you'd have chosen the piano or the violin. I myself can hardly read music; I rely much more on listening to a tune and then humming and singing along in order to find my way. With that in mind, in this guide we'll learn to play the ukulele with pictures and letters, and hopefully have a jolly good time along the way.

So let's assume that you know nothing about music, or ukuleles. Imagine you are a blank slate, a shapeless lump of clay, about to form yourself into a beautiful sculpture. The ukulele is an easy instrument to learn, and it soon rewards your efforts. Very soon you'll be singing and playing lots of tunes, and it won't have been a struggle. The most important thing to remember is to have fun with it and not to get bogged down. Take your time. If at any point you're finding anything tricky, go and have a cup of tea.

QUICK-START GUIDE TO PLAYING THE UKULELE

If I buy a new appliance, there's often a 'Quick Start' section in the instructions. I love these sections, because I am impatient to a fault. I thought it'd be good to have a 'Quick Start' section in this book for those of you who already know a little bit about music or who, like me, are just too impatient to take it slowly.

So here goes - ten easy steps to playing the ukulele...

1

Get hold of a soprano ukulele. Don't spend too much on it.

2

Tune the strings to GCEA (G above middle C, middle C, E above middle C, A above middle C). This will make it sound easy on the ear (see pages 94 and 98).

3

Hold the neck of the uke in your left hand and strum the strings with your right. This will enable you to sing with your mouth while you tap your toes and jiggle your knees.

4

Learn some chords. This is an example of a chord box: Chord boxes represent the four strings and the first four frets of the uke. The dots are where your fingers go. The numbers show which fingers to use.

5

Look in a songbook or on the internet and find the chords and lyrics to a groovy song that you want to play.

6

Flip to the back of this book where you will find our handy pull-out ukulele chord chart to find out what the chord shapes you need look like.

7

Write these chord boxes onto the music. This will make it easy to get strumming.

8

Strum the song and don't forget to sing out!

9

Find another song and go back to step six.

10

Make a nice cup of tea. For the rest of you, read on...

GET A UKULELE

To play the ukulele, you'll need to get hold of one - this is an unavoidable part of learning the instrument. Before you do, though, there are a few things you should consider.

WHICH SIZE?

You may be surprised to hear that there is more than one size of ukulele. Indeed, just like the people who pluck them, the ukulele comes in a variety of different sizes. Strangely, they are pretty much all tuned and played in the same way.

The different sizes of ukulele range all the way from bass to fridge magnet, although by far the best known is the soprano.

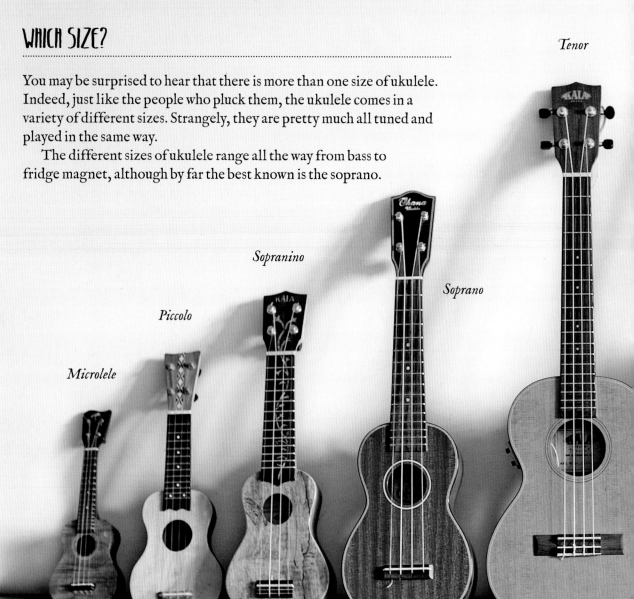

Tenor

Sopranino

Piccolo

Soprano

Microlele

Baritone

Bass

Microlele

This one is more of a fridge magnet to be honest, a rare collectors' piece made by Tangi Ukuleles that's almost playable. It also makes good kindling for a ukulele bonfire.

Piccolo and Sopranino ukuleles

I am a big fan of the piccolo and sopranino ukuleles - ukes you really can fit in your pocket. They are recent additions to the ukulele family and tend to get tuned an octave above a soprano. This means you can play the same chord shapes on them, but you will attract more dogs. Not long ago these were only available as handmade

instruments, but now it's possible to buy off-the-peg piccolo ukuleles that sound great. As they have a smaller fretboard, you may find it tricky to fit your sausage fingers around them, so these are not ukes to get started on. Definitely something for your expanding collection, though.

Soprano ukulele

This is the 'classic' ukulele, and probably the best ukulele for you to get started on. If you're in any doubt at all, get a soprano. It's the most common size - it will fit snugly under you arm, and also has the advantage of fitting neatly into a wastepaper basket, should you ever tire of it.

Tenor (and Concert) ukuleles

Tenor (and the smaller concert) ukuleles have larger bodies and longer necks than sopranos but are tuned the same, making them perfect for those who have issues with small instruments.

Baritone ukulele

The baritone ukulele is tuned slightly lower than a soprano. This means that it doesn't have that classic plinky ukulele sound, although that can make a welcome addition to a group of ukuleles, as it brings mid-ranging notes that otherwise wouldn't be there. The one pictured on page 89 is actually a Venezuelan ukulele called a cuatro. It's the same size as a baritone ukulele, and I've tuned it up like one. The baritone can also be a good ukulele to pick up if you already know some guitar, as it's exactly the same as a guitar

that is missing two strings (the two lowest ones, nearest your nose as you play it). It's essentially a tenor guitar (a small guitar), but rechristened as a baritone ukulele (a big ukulele).

Bass ukulele

There's some debate as to what a bass ukulele is - it's not a 'traditional' uke, but a modern invention. In my view, any ukulele-shaped acoustic bass is better described as a bass ukulele, because it has four strings (see picture, page 89). Four fingers, four strings. Ukulele.

Basses nearly always have four strings, and guitars have six, so 'bass guitars' aren't really guitars at all. Other than being a similar shape to a guitar, they are more like the double bass, which we know from classical orchestras and jazz bands. They're tuned in the same way, as well.

These days you can buy instruments called bass ukuleles, but the only difference between these and acoustic basses is they're smaller and tend to have rubbery strings. But remember, basses aren't 'chord' instruments - instead, people play single notes on them, which gives a nice 'bottom end' to any band.

Banjo-ukulele

In the early 20th century, instrument makers very often stuck a banjo body onto any instrument they could lay their hands on, creating banjo-guitars, mandolin-banjos (banjolins) and other weird hybrids. The banjo-ukulele, or banjolele, is the ukulele that most of us would associate with George Formby (see pages 24-7). This is tuned the same as a soprano ukulele, and played in the same way, but the body is shaped like a small banjo, with the bridge sitting on something like the skin of a drum. It gives a very loud, banjo-ey sound and will make a great addition to your ukulele collection once you've really got the bug.

Opposite: The Everyman ukulele – a soprano.

Below: A 'Keech' banjo-ukulele – this one's been signed by Duke Ellington, no less.

SHRUNKEN GUITAR OR OVERGROWN UKULELE?

The guitar and the ukulele do have an awful lot in common. Anyone with some experience of playing guitar will quickly realize that the chord shapes on a ukulele are very similar to those on the top four strings of a guitar, although they have different names. Look at the picture of a guitar on the right.

If we rip off the two lowest strings, tune one of the strings an octave higher and put our finger across the strings on the fifth fret, we have a ukulele. A monstrous ukulele, but a ukulele nonetheless. So all the shapes you know for a guitar - say, a G chord - become five semitones higher. In the case of a G shape, it becomes a C chord. Easy, eh?

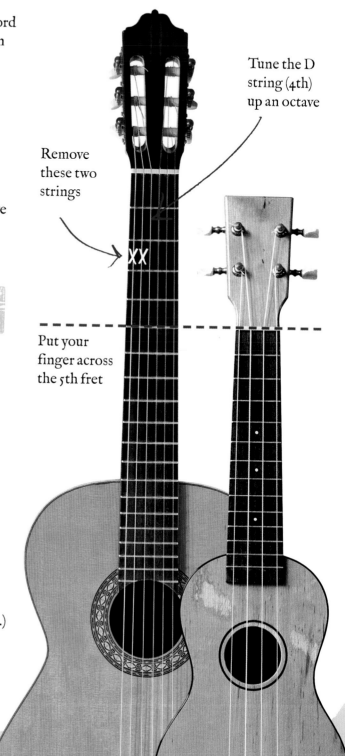

Tune the D string (4th) up an octave

Remove these two strings

XX

Put your finger across the 5th fret

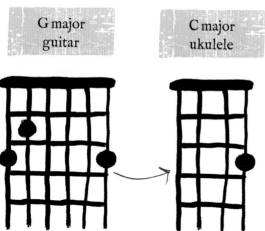

| G major guitar | C major ukulele |

Now all you have to do is learn the new names for all your guitar chords, and you can throw this book away. (And once you know all the new ukulele chords, you can throw your guitar away, making space for a few more ukes.)

WHAT TO LOOK FOR IN A UKULELE

These days the wannabe plucker has a staggering array of ukuleles to choose from. A quick search online will produce a tidal wave of ukulele options and this can often be the novice's first stumbling block. Which one do I pick? When I first started playing, there were only one or two brands available, so the decision was made easier, but these days we have to plunge in and be selective.

Below are a few things to be sure of when buying your first ukulele.

 Your ukulele has geared tuning pegs (which stick out of the side of the head), rather than friction pegs (which come out of the back of the head). Geared tuning pegs are better at keeping the strings in tune and if your uke keeps going out of tune it sounds rubbish.

 You like it.

 It sounds okay.

 Erm, that's all I can think of.

Some brands I could recommend are Kala (or Makala), Lanikai, Ohana, KoAloha, Bushman, Bruko and Pono ukuleles. All these ukes are well built and most have the geared tuning pegs as standard. Don't limit yourself to these brands, though - there are lots of extremely good makers out there, and most modern ukuleles sound okay.

Right: This is what my Martin ukulele looks like after over 20 years of strumming - holey. It's worth mentioning the Konter Martin Ukulele, which was the first instrument to travel over the North Pole - Dick Konter smuggled it aboard Robert Byrd's 1926 exploratory flight from Spitzbergen.

HOW MUCH TO SPEND

A good beginner's ukulele shouldn't cost you more than £40, but you can spend anything from £20-10,000 on a uke. They are addictive - if you enjoy playing the ukulele, you may want to buy another. Buy a cheaper one to get started and if you don't like it you can use it as a bird box.

Of course, the canny cash-laden plucker could invest in a vintage ukulele. Apart from the vast array of beautifully made Hawaiian ukuleles out there, of which there are too many builders to name, some of the biggest guitar companies in the world started out making ukuleles, and these are particularly sought-after. Gibson, best known for their electric guitars, made beautiful ukuleles in the 1920s and 1930s, and Martin, another renowned guitar manufacturer, produced thousands of fantastic ukuleles, which far outnumbered their guitar production at the time.

WHERE TO BUY IT

These days you can buy a ukulele straight from the internet, but if at all possible I'd recommend going to a music shop and having a go on a ukulele before you buy it - nearly every music shop out there will have a few ukuleles you can try. The weight, feel and look of a ukulele are all things you'll want to assess. Indeed, you may find that the tenor ukulele fits your fingers better, or that your beer belly gets in the way of the soprano. You'll never know until you try it.

WHICH WOOD?

People often ask what kind of wood gives the best sound for a ukulele. The traditional Hawaiian ukes were made from koa wood, which has a beautiful grain to it and makes for a nice mellow sound, but only if the uke has been well built. I'd be hard-pressed to say that one wood gives a 'better' sound than another. The sound has much more to do with the way the instrument has been built and the way it's played than what it's been made out of. I've heard people murder a tune on a £5,000 uke, while others can make a piece of plywood sing like an angel. I've played mahogany ukes, koa ukes, plywood ukes, plastic ukes, even a stained-glass uke, and each of them had their own unique and special quality.

The best thing to do is to find a ukulele that suits you. I subscribe to the philosophy that it's a uke - an inexpensive, fun instrument - so it wants to sound like an inexpensive, fun instrument. Much better to have a ukulele that you can lose and not shed a tear for than a priceless Martin that you leave on a train on your way home from school. I should know (see page 10).

Above: Ukuleles are now produced all over the world. This chap is whittling away in the central Philippine city of Cebu, where there's been a recent boom in uke sales.

EXTRAS

Tuner
Now you have your ukulele, you'll need to keep it in tune, and for this you'll need an electronic tuner. You *can* tune a ukulele by ear, but this nifty little gadget does it all for you. You simply clip the tuner onto the top of your uke head, pluck the strings in turn and it tells you when each one is in tune (see page 98 for instructions on how to tune). You can buy these in any music shop and they are an absolutely indispensable bit of kit. Remember, all ukuleles go out

of tune, so if it starts to sound rubbish, it's probably not you. Time to check your tuning.

Strings

A good set of strings can make all the difference to the sound of a cheap uke. Occasionally a ukulele will arrive strung with such awful strings that the poor plucker won't have a hope of keeping them in tune. In such cases, Aquila, D'Addario and Worth are some respected ukulele string manufacturers, but there are lots of different options out there. (See page 166-7 for instructions on how to change your ukulele strings.) It should also be noted that any thin, fibrous material can be used as a string. George Hinchliffe of the Ukulele Orchestra of Great Britain uses coarse fishing line for his top string and it sounds great.

Plectrums

Now, ukulele purists may hate me for this, but I think it's okay to strum your ukulele with a plectrum. Really. No problem. The traditional way of playing is to use your fingertips, but if you find it easier to use a plectrum, why not? Ukulele 'experts' often get very upset about this, but in general these are people who like to hang their ukuleles on the wall and not play them too much.

The truth is you can use either. If you want to use a plectrum, you're better off using a harder guitar pick, not a floppy plastic one, as they can sound clacky. Alternatively, you can use a soft felt plectrum, which gives the uke a mellow, muffled sound, perfect for quiet practice and thoughtful strumming.

I have pretty tough nails, so I've grown three of mine on my right hand - kind of grow-your-own plectrums. The disadvantage of this (if you're a man) is that it makes you look a bit creepy, but on the plus side you're never without them. If you have easily breakable nails, you can always get some false ones. There are a number of websites that sell great false nails for guitarists, which work just as well for ukulelists.

In short, you should feel free to use whatever suits you: nail, flesh or plastic. It's a ukulele, and we're here to have fun with it.

A Case

If you've spent money on your ukulele, it's worth getting a case to keep it safe. There are hard and soft cases out there, but I'd recommend a good hard case, so that you can drop your ukulele without fear of breaking it. The little hard cases also have the advantage of making you look like a very unthreatening gangster packing an unimpressive gun.

UKULELE ACQUISITION SYNDROME

At this stage, you should be warned: ukuleles are the crack cocaine of musical instruments. There is no such thing as owning just one. If you enjoy playing the ukulele, you will undoubtedly find yourself wondering if you might buy just one more, and it can be exceedingly difficult to keep this purchasing habit under control. It can mean that your ukulele collection grows at an alarming rate. I fondly remember the day when

I had just one ukulele, but at the last count I have 36 cluttering the shelves and floors of my house. I'm not quite sure where they all came from, or how I will ever get rid of them, but they appear to be here to stay.

Below: Displayed here is a mere fraction of my friend UkeHeidi's ukulele collection. How he manages to get into his house, I really have no idea.

FIRST TENTATIVE STEPS

HOLD IT

There are many schools of thought on the 'correct' way to hold a ukulele. I tend to think that you should hold it how you want to hold it, so that you feel comfortable. Some say it must not be rested on your lap, but tucked underneath your arm; some recommend you use a strap, while others think the ukulele sounds best stamped underfoot.

With a bit of experimentation, you will find what suits you best. This is a ukulele, not a Stradivarius, so you should feel free from the baggage of thousands of years of experts' opinions and do what you like.

If you're going to play a tune, though, there are some essentials you can't avoid. Sitting on it, for example, will not produce a good sound (although some may disagree).

The basic way to hold a ukulele is (for right-handed people) to rest the neck of your ukulele in your left hand, so you can strum the strings with your right (see above right). If you're left-handed, hold the neck with the right hand and strum with your left. (If you want to play your ukulele left-handed, see pages 102-3 for ideas on how to get started.)

I like to play sitting down with my ukulele sitting on my lap, but to play it standing up, one can employ a variety of methods. I tend to use an old shoelace tied around the uke body underneath the strings and then looped around my neck, which is extremely effective, but if you want something a bit posher, you can get hold of innumerable fancy ukulele straps these days on the internet. Perhaps the simplest way to learn to play standing up is just to tuck the body of the uke underneath your right forearm, while strumming it from your wrist. That way, you won't ever have to bother with a strap. To master this technique, the thing to remember is to relax, not squeeze it too tightly, and try to allow your left hand some freedom to move up and down the fretboard.

TUNE IT

The ukulele has an eccentric kind of tuning. The notes do not run from low to high. Instead, the lowest string on a ukulele is the second one away from your nose. This eccentricity gives guitar and violin players the horrors when they try a ukulele out - 'What IS this thing?' - but don't let it alarm you. It's part of what gives the ukulele its cheerful character, and it's called re-entrant tuning.

Getting your ukulele in tune is VERY important. It's really the key to playing the ukulele properly. If it's not in tune, it will put you off the whole idea, so pay close attention to this bit...

There are many different ways to tune a ukulele but the most common tuning is GCEA (for other ideas on how to tune your uke, see pages 152-3) This means that the string closest to your nose is tuned to a G (the one just above middle C on a piano), the next is a C (middle C) and finally E and A (both above middle C). Below are the notes on a piano.

You can tune your ukulele by ear if you have a piano nearby. Otherwise, now is the moment to clip on your electronic tuner and let it do its magic. To tune each string, you need to twist the tuning peg that the string is attached to (see above). Tightening the string will make the note go higher; loosening it will make the note go lower (just like when you twang a rubber band).

If you elected to ignore my earlier advice and have bought a ukulele with friction pegs (rather than geared tuning pegs - see page 93), you may find that the screws in the back of the pegs need to be tightened up to stop the strings from slipping. Just take a screwdriver and tighten the screws (see opposite, top) so you can still twist the peg but it stays firmly in place once you let go.

TUNING A UKULELE TO ITSELF

If you have no electronic tuner and no other instrument to help you, then you'll have to tune your ukulele to itself. It may not be in tune with any other instruments, but it'll sound okay and will let you get on with some practice.

First, tighten up the C string so that it is firm and taut and sounds nice and bright.

Now put your finger on the fourth fret of the C string, pluck that note and tune the E string to that same note.

Once that's in tune, place your finger on the fifth fret of the E string and tune the A string to that note.

Finally play the third fret of the E string and tune the G string to that note. To be sure your strings are in tune, check that the second fret of the G string is playing the same note as the open A string. With any luck, your ukulele is now in tune.

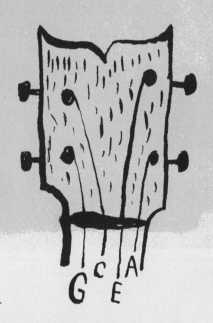

STRUM IT

To strum your instrument, take your right forefinger and brush it gently downwards across the strings, just above the sound hole. This should already sound quite nice. In fact, you've just played your first chord - it's an Am$_7$ (A minor seventh), and also a C^6 (C sixth), so you can feel pretty pleased with yourself already. Easy-peasy.

My friend Mara Carlyle wrote a great song called 'Baby Bloodheart' using (almost) only this chord. So, if you want, you can stop right here, and instead get busy writing some lyrics to your own songs. Who needs to learn chord shapes anyway?

PLAYING CHORDS

★ ★ ★ ★ ★ ★ ★ ★ ★ ★ ★ ★ ★ ★ ★ ★

THE FIRST CHORD (C) AND CHORD BOXES

The ukulele is a brilliant instrument to play chords on. A chord is a group of different notes, all played at the same time, that sound good together. Luckily for us the ukulele has four strings and we have four fingers to use so life will never get too complicated.

A simple way for ukulele chords to be displayed is by using chord boxes. These are graphic representations of the first few frets of the neck of the ukulele, and they show you where to put your fingers to make a chord. The up-and-down lines represent the strings, and the side-to-side lines represent the frets. So to play the chord of C, we would write a chord box that looks like the one below.

If this doesn't make sense, just take your ukulele and place a finger on the third fret of the A string (the one furthest from your nose - see below). This is a C chord. If you compare this to the chord box, it should begin to make sense.

What you're doing when you put your finger on the third fret is shortening the string length, which in turn makes the note higher. If it sounds buzzy, make sure you're pressing down firmly, just behind the third fret. You need to push down on the string to get a clear note. Let it know who's boss.

We've added numbers on the black dots in the chord boxes. These are suggestions for which finger to use. Number 1 is your pointing finger, number 2 is your middle finger, number 3 is your ring finger and number 4 is your little finger. To make life easier later on, it's good if you can learn to use your third (ring) finger for the C chord as it'll make changing chords a lot easier.

You've now learned your first Major chord, and it's a C. This is a great chord to know because we use it a lot, and it's very easy to play.

Have a cup of tea. Don't rush it. Things are going well so you deserve a nice cup of tea.

PLAYING LEFT-HANDED

If you are left-handed, you are probably noticing as you read through this section that it takes a predominantly right-handed approach to the ukulele, but don't let this put you off. Left-handed players can easily play the ukulele. Of course, some left-handed players simply learn to play right-handed and, if you're just starting, you may like to try this out and see how it suits you.

Another option is simply to turn the ukulele around (so you strum with the left hand, and form chord shapes with the right) - it worked for Tiny Tim and Ian Whitcomb, both left-handed ukulele icons. The downside of this approach is that the strings will now be upside down, running AECG, so you'll have to find new ways to finger the chords.

If you do decide to hold the ukulele left-handed, you may prefer to re-string your ukulele (see pages 166-7), so the string that was at the top is now at the bottom. This means that the strings will still run GCEA (from nose to floor), as with a right-handed ukulele. The side-effect of re-stringing your uke is that the chord boxes won't work, so you will have to 'mirror image' them, as shown in the illustrations on the right.

F CHORD

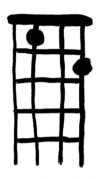

right-handed   *left-handed*

C CHORD

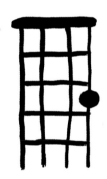

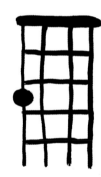

right-handed   *left-handed*

Tiny Tim played ukulele left-handed, just like Paul McCartney, Dick Dale and Jimi Hendrix. Plaid jackets, however, are optional.

STRUMMING IN TIME

When you play music, it's important to play on the beat. Most pop music has a 4/4 beat, which means there are four beats in every bar. This is why you often hear people saying, 'A-one, a-two, a-one, two, three, four', to count in a groovy tune. So by thinking of music as evenly spaced groups of four beats, we can begin to get going.

Using the end of your right forefinger (or a plectrum, if you prefer), gently stroke the strings, strumming from your wrist rather than your elbow. Getting into the habit of strumming from your wrist will help you later on. Strumming from your elbow (and keeping your wrist rigid) is quite a workout and can become extremely exhausting, and that's the last thing we want. Whatever you do, don't work too hard.

We can split the basic ukulele strum into two strokes: the downstroke (when your finger moves down across the strings) and the upstroke (when your finger moves up across the strings).

Let's split our four beats up, and think of them as: 1 donk, 2 donk, 3 donk, 4 donk. Try using the downstroke and the upstroke simply by alternating each one. Play the downstroke on each 1, 2, 3, 4, and the upstroke on the 4 donks.

WHERE TO STRUM?

There are lots of different sounds you can get out of your ukulele. To get a nice ukulele-type sound from it, you should aim to strum around the bottom of the fretboard, just above the sound hole.

You'll find the higher up the strings you strum, the more mellow the sound will become. If you strum right over the higher frets you should hear the sound quality change to a quieter, more gentle sound.

If you want to get a harder, rockier sound from your uke, you need to strum further down the strings, towards the bridge. This will produce a harsher sound that may not be that nice on its own but can be used to great effect in part of a song or to beef up a chorus.

A BASIC STRUM

1 *donk*	**2** *donk*	**3** *donk*	**4** *donk*
DOWN UP	DOWN UP	DOWN UP	DOWN UP

1

Remember to strum from the wrist. On your marks, get set...

2

Strum down across the strings. Sounds nice, hey?

3

Pull your finger back up across the strings and you're back where you started. Repeat!

SONGS
TO STRUM
ALONG TO

(AND SOME CHORDS TO LEARN
AT THE SAME TIME)

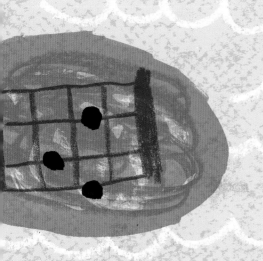

PLAYING A ONE-CHORD SONG

★ ★

Okay, hold onto your hats, because it's already time for you to try to play a tune. Happily, there are quite a few songs out there that require you to know only one chord. You'll be pleased to hear that they're the ones we'll get started on, so you can get used to strumming a bit.

We can use the C chord that you've just learned (see pages 100-1, and below) to play a whole song, and it's a very simple kids' tune, 'Row, Row, Row Your Boat'. By counting a steady 1, 2, 3, 4 rhythm as you sing the song, you'll find that certain words fall on certain beats. Here is the song written out in beats.

1	2	3	4
Row	row	row your	boat
Gently	down the	stream	
Merrily	merrily	merrily	merrily
Life is	but a	dream	

★ ★ ★ ★ ★ ★ ★ ★ ★ ★ ★ ★ ★ ★ ★

PLAY ALONG WITH THE SONGS ONLINE

Every song in this book is available to listen to and play along with on my website: www.willgrovewhite.com. Once you're there, just click the *Get Plucky* button and you'll be able to strum along to each tune with me. This is a really handy way to learn, especially if you're unfamiliar with any of the songs.

★ ★ ★ ★ ★ ★ ★ ★ ★ ★ ★ ★ ★ ★ ★ ★

The first challenge is to put two elements together: singing and playing. Play four strums for each line of the tune (one strum of your C chord for each beat), and sing the tune while you do it. The first note to sing is a C (the second string from your nose), for 'Row...'.

'Frère Jacques' will work equally well using this one chord (see below). This French lullaby has to be one of the most well-known songs in the Western world. I've always been tickled by the way that 'dang' is spelt in this song - 'daing'. It reminds me of the Beverly Hillbillies.

Just like 'Row, Row, Row Your Boat,' the first note to sing for Frère Jacques is a C.

1	2	3	4	1	2	3	4
Frè-	re	Jac-	ques	Frè-	re	Jac-	ques
C	-	-	-	C	-	-	-
Dor-	mez	vous?		Dor-	mez	vous?	
C	-	-	-	C	-	-	-
Sonnez	les ma-	ti-	nes	Sonnez	les ma-	ti-	nes
C	-	-	-	C	-	-	-
Ding	daing	dong		Ding	daing	dong	
C	-	-	-	C	-	-	-

A GROOVIER ONE-CHORD SONG

C7

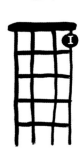

Another great one-chord song to try is 'Baby Please Don't Go,' an old blues song that has been performed by almost everyone, from Muddy Waters to AC/DC via Van Morrison (when he was in the band Them). If you don't know the tune, you can hear it and buy it online. This whole song can be played using only a C7 chord (although if you want to play along with Them's version you'll need to play an F7). Seventh chords sound more 'bluesy' than major chords. In the case of C7, just use your first finger on the first fret of the A string, like this.

Right: As you play through this book, you may find it useful to draw the chord boxes next to the chord names in the music. The act of drawing the boxes will help you to remember the chord shapes.

Now you can play this tune using one finger. The first notes to sing are E♭ (flat), C, E♭ for 'Baby please...' (see the diagram of notes on the fretboard on page 149 to find these notes on your ukulele).

BABY PLEASE DON'T GO

2 3 4	1	2	3	4	1	2	3	4
Baby please don't	go					Baby	please	don't
	C7	-	-	-	C7	-	-	-
	please	don't	go	back to	New Or-		leans you	know I
	C7	-	-	-	C7	-	-	-

BABY PLEASE DON'T GO

Baby please don't go,
Baby please don't go,
Baby please don't go, back to New Orleans,
You know I love you so, baby please don't go.

You know your man done gone,
You know your man done gone,
You know your man done gone, to the
country farm,
With all the shackles on, baby please don't go.

You know I'm way down here,
You know I'm way down here,
You know I'm way down here, in a rolling fog,
They treat me like a dog, baby please don't go.

Baby please don't go,
Baby please don't go,
Baby, please don't go, and leave me here,
You know it's cold down here,
baby please don't go.

MORE ONE-CHORD SONGS

So why bother learning how to change chords?
I love one-chord songs. If you like the idea of
playing songs with only one chord, there are a
whole heap of them:

☞ Harry Nilsson's 'Coconut' is all played
on a C_7 chord.
☞ Aretha Franklin's 'Chain of Fools' is
also all on the C_7 chord.
☞ 'The Clapping Song', made famous by
Shirley Ellis in the 1960s, is all on an
C_7 chord.
☞ Sonny and Cher's 'The Beat Goes On'
uses only an F chord.
☞ Bob Marley's 'Exodus' is all on an A
minor chord, and 'Get Up, Stand Up' is
all on a C minor chord.
☞ Another great one is Bob Dylan's
'Ballad of Hollis Brown', which only uses
a D minor chord throughout.

You can find all these songs on the internet
if you want to play along, and all of these chord
shapes can be found on the handy pull-out
ukulele chord dictionary at the back of this book.

1	2	3	4	1	2	3	4
go							Baby
C_7	-	-	-	C_7	-	-	-
love	you so		Baby	please	don't	go	
C_7	-	-	-	C_7	-	-	-

IT'S TIME FOR ANOTHER CHORD

For those of you who are ready for more and want to learn another chord, here goes. The next one is F, and the chord box looks like this:

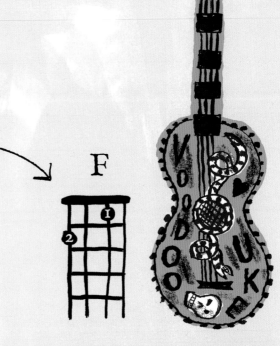

F

The easiest way to play this is to use your forefinger on the E string, and your middle finger on the G string, as in the picture below.

It may seem as if your fingers will never learn how to get into this position, but they will - it just takes a little practice. What you're aiming to do is put the C and the F chord together, so you can learn a song.

SONGS WITH TWO CHORDS – C AND F

There are heaps of songs you can play using just two chords. Because nursery rhymes are nice and simple, let's try another kids' song. This time it's 'London Bridge Is Falling Down'. This is one of the oldest tunes in the book, dating back to the 17th century, maybe even earlier. The first note to sing is a C (the second string from your nose) for 'Lon...'.

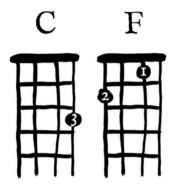

LONDON BRIDGE IS FALLING DOWN

(F) London Bridge is falling down,
(C) Falling down, (F) falling down,
London Bridge is falling down,
(C) My fair (F) lady.

(F) Build it up with wood and clay,
(C) Wood and clay, (F) wood and clay,
Build it up with wood and clay,
(C) My fair (F) lady.

(F) Wood and clay will wash away,
(C) Wash away, (F) wash away,
Wood and clay will wash away,
(C) My fair (F) lady.

(F) Build it up with iron and steel,
(C) Iron and steel, (F) iron and steel,
Build it up with iron and steel,
(C) My fair (F) lady.

LONDON BRIDGE IS FALLING DOWN

1	2	3	4	1	2	3	4
Lon-	don	Bridge	is	fall-	ing	down	
F	-	-	-	**F**	-	-	-
Fall-	ing	down		Fall-	ing	down	
C	-	-	-	**F**	-	-	-
Lon-	don	Bridge	is	fall-	ing	down	
F	-	-	-	**F**	-	-	-
My		fair		La-	dy		
C	-	-	-	**F**	-	-	-

A much groovier tune you can try with these two chords is 'Down in the Valley'. This is also a traditional American folk tune, but is better known sung by both Solomon Burke and Otis Redding. Have a listen to it online if you've not heard it before. Just use the F and C chord as you strum along. The first note to sing is an F for 'Down in…'.

DOWN IN THE VALLEY

Down in the (F) valley, the valley so (C) low,
Hang your head over, hear the wind (F) blow,
Hear the wind blow, dear, hear the wind (C) blow;
Hang your head over, in the valley so (F) low.

Roses love (F) sunshine, violets love (C) dew,
Angels in Heaven know I love (F) you,
Know I love you, dear, know I love (C) you,
Angels in Heaven know I love (F) you.

If you don't (F) love me, love whom you (C) please,
Throw your arms round me, give my heart (F) ease,
Give my heart ease, dear, give my heart (C) ease,
Throw your arms round me, give my heart (F) ease.

Build me a (F) castle, forty feet (C) high;
So I can see her as she rides (F) by,
As she rides by, dear, as she rides (C) by,
So I can see her as she rides (F) by.

DOWN IN THE VALLEY

3 4	1	2	3	4	1	2	3	4 —
Down in the	val-	ley				the	valley	so
	F	-	-	-	F	-	-	-
	o-	ver					hear the	wind
	C	-	-	-	C	-	-	-
	blow	dear					hear the	wind
	F	-	-	-	F	-	-	-
	o-	ver				in the	valley	so
	C	-	-	-	C	-	-	-

CHANGING CHORDS

A good way to get your fingers used to changing between the C and F chords is to practise playing four strums on C, and then four strums on F, while trying to keep the rhythm steady as you change between the two. Because you're using your third finger for the C chord, and your first and second fingers for the F chord, it should be a (fairly) straightforward move.

Try to make it a smooth transition between the chords. When changing from a C to an F, have your first and second fingers ready above the places they'll sit for the F chord. While you're playing the F chord you'll notice that your ring finger is already positioned over the 3rd fret where it needs to land for the C. Clever eh?

It really doesn't matter how slowly you go to begin with, but getting used to changing chords is the KEY to playing the ukulele. Just don't rush! Keep practising, and remember to take breaks in between. Stopping practice for a bit is NOT giving up; it's an important part of the process. While you're busy doing something else, your brain will be going over what you've just learned, so you'll find that every time you come back to practise again, you'll be able to change chords a little quicker, until you can do it without your tongue sticking out of the side of your mouth like an idiot.

→ 1	2	3	4	1	2	3	4
low						Hang your	head
C	-	-	-	C	-	-	-
blow						Hear the	wind
F	-	-	-	F	-	-	-
blow						Hang your	head
C	-	-	-	C	-	-	-
low							
F	-	-	-	F	-	-	-

A THIRD CHORD – G7

The vast majority of rock, blues, reggae and pop music is based around three chords. In the key of C, these chords are C, F and G. Now that you've learned C and F, you're two-thirds of the way towards knowing about a million songs, so don't give up now - you're well on the way to being able to play a vast repertoire of songs with which to delight and amuse (or drive out of your house) your friends and relations.

The third chord to try is a G_7, **G7** and you'll see to the right what the chord box looks like.

The easiest way to play this is to use your forefinger on the E string, your middle finger on the C string and your third finger on the A string, like in the picture, top right.

Now give it a strum. Again, you must practise changing chords. From the G_7 position you should find it quite easy to slide your 3rd finger along the A string to get it in position to play the C chord. In the next songs you'll just be using C and G_7, so have a go at changing between these two chords - again, try four strums on each chord and then change position. Go slowly! If it helps (and you know it does) try having a sip of tea in between each strum.

OH MY DARLING CLEMENTINE

3	I	2	3
In a	cav-	ern	in a
	C	-	-
	min-	er,	forty-
	G_7	-	-
	dar-	ling	oh my
	C	-	-
	lost	and	gone for-
	G_7	-	-

TWO-CHORD SONGS WITH C AND G7

Once you feel ready, have a go at this American folk tune, 'Oh My Darling Clementine'. At first glance, the song appears to be a tragic ballad about a bereaved lover, but as the long procession of verses progresses it turns out to have quite a few funny lines, one referring to Clem's enormous feet.

Tom Lehrer's version is great fun. He theorizes that folk songs are 'atrocious because they're written by the people' and so he re-imagines 'Oh My Darling Clementine' as written by Cole Porter, Mozart and modern jazzers. But we won't try that just yet. This is a very simple tune to play, and the first note to sing is a C for 'In a...'.

OH MY DARLING CLEMENTINE

In a (C) cavern, in a canyon,
Excavating for a (G7) mine,
Dwelt a miner forty- (C) niner,
And his (G7) daughter Clemen- (C) tine.

CHORUS
Oh my (C) darling, oh my darling,
Oh my darling, Clemen- (G7) tine!
You are lost and gone for- (C) ever,
Oh my (G7) darling, Clemen- (C) tine.

Drove she (C) ducklings to the water,
Every morning just at (G7) nine,
Hit her foot against a (C) splinter,
Fell in (G7) to the foaming (C) brine.

REPEAT CHORUS

Ruby (C) lips above the water,
Blowing bubbles, soft and (G7) fine,
But, alas, I was no (C) swimmer,
So I (G7) lost my Clemen- (C) tine.

→ 1	2	3	1	2	3	1	2	3
can-	yon	Exca-	va-	ting	for a	mine		Dwelt a
C	-	-	C	-	-	G7	-	-
ni-	ner	And his	daugh-	ter	Clemen-	tine		Oh my
C	-	-	G7	-	-	C	-	-
dar-	ling	Oh my	dar-	ling	Clemen-	tine!		You are
C	-	-	C	-	-	G7	-	-
ev-	er	Oh my	dar-	ling	Clemen-	tine.		
C	-	-	G7	-	-	C	-	-

A classic spiritual tune that can be played with C and G$_7$ is 'He's Got the Whole World in His Hands'. The astonishingly voiced Mahalia Jackson recorded this one as well as, less notably, Nottingham Forest FC (with Paper Lace). It's become a favourite at football grounds, where fans often adapt the lyrics. Rushden & Diamonds fans have been heard to sing, 'We're the Worst Team in the League' to the tune of this song. The first note to sing is a G for 'He's got…'.

HE'S GOT THE WHOLE WORLD IN HIS HANDS

3 4	1	2	3	4	1	2	3	4
He's got the	whole		world		in	His	hands He's	got the
	C	-	-	-	C	-	-	-
	whole		world		in	His	hands He's	got the
	G$_7$	-	-	-	G$_7$	-	-	-
	whole		world		in	His	hands He's	got the
	C	-	-	-	C	-	-	-
	whole	world	in	His	hands			
	G$_7$	-	-	-	C	-	-	-

HE'S GOT THE WHOLE WORLD IN HIS HANDS

He's got the (C) whole world in His hands,
He's got the (G$_7$) whole world in His hands,
He's got the (C) whole world in His hands,
He's got the (G$_7$) whole world in His (C) hands.

He's got everybody here in His hands (×4)

He's got the little bitty baby in His hands (×4)

He's got the whole world in His hands (×4)

MORE C AND G7 TUNES TO TRY

☛ A couple of other wonderful songs that can be played with C and G$_7$ are 'Iko Iko', a Grateful Dead and Dr John staple, as well as Hank Williams' Cajun-style country tune 'Jambalaya (On the Bayou)'. 'Singin' in the Rain', a tune originally popularized by Cliff Edwards ('Ukulele Ike') is another C and G$_7$ song. Start 'Singin' in the Rain' by playing a C chord - for 'I'm sing…' and change to the G$_7$ on the word 'happy'. Then try and listen for the changes - it's all on those two chords.

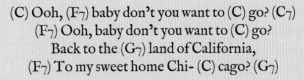

SWEET HOME CHICAGO

(C) Ooh, (F7) baby don't you want to (C) go? (C7)
(F7) Ooh, baby don't you want to (C) go?
Back to the (G7) land of California,
(F7) To my sweet home Chi- (C) cago? (G7)

Now (C) one and one is two, (F7) two and two is four,
(C) I'm heavy loaded baby, (C7) I gotta go,
I'm cryin' (F7) baby, honey don't you want to (C) go?
Back to the (G7) land of California, (F7) my sweet home Chi- (C) cago? (G7)

Now (C) two and two is four, (F7) four and two is six,
(C) You keep monkeying around, you gonna get (C7) all in a trick,
I'm cryin' (F7) baby, honey don't you wanna (C) go?
Back to the (G7) land of California, (F7) my sweet home Chi- (C) cago. (G7)

SWEET HOME CHICAGO

I	2	3	4	I	2	3	4
Ooh				baby	don't you	want	to
C	-	-	-	F7	-	-	-
go?							
C	-	-	-	C7	-	-	-
Ooh				baby	don't you	want	to
F7	-	-	-	F7	-	-	-
go?						Back	to the
C	-	-	-	C	-	-	-
land of	Cali-	fornia		To my	sweet	home	Chi-
G7	-	-	-	F7	-	-	-
cago							
C	-	-	-	G7	-	-	-

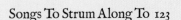

SOME NEW CHORDS AND TUNES

We've already seen how 'Amazing Grace,' 'Twist and Shout' and 'Wild Thing' only use three chords (the 1: 4: 5 chords), so let's try out some more songs, but this time in different keys, to get your fingers used to some more shapes. For this, you're going to need a few more chords, but they're not too tricky, so don't fret. They're A, D, E7 and G. See the pictures below for how to play them.

We'll kick off with these new chords by learning one of the most famous American gospel tunes there is, 'When The Saints Go Marching In'. Louis Armstrong popularized this tune in the 1930s, and it's become a staple of performers ever since, from Fats Domino and Judy Garland to Bruce Springsteen. The unofficial anthem of New Orleans, it's become so notorious that many jazz players demand extra incentives to perform it. These days in

New Orleans' most famous jazz venue, Preservation Hall, requests for tunes are priced at $5 a pop. But 'The Saints' will cost you $20. Hopefully *you* don't need bribing, though!

The first notes to sing are A, C# (sharp), D for 'Oh when the...'.

WHEN THE SAINTS GO MARCHING IN

Oh when the (A) saints go marching in,
When the saints go marching (E7) in,
I want to (A) be in that (D) number,
When the (A) saints go (E7) marching (A) in.

Oh when the (A) sun begins to shine,
Oh when the sun begins to (E7) shine,
I want to (A) be in that (D) number,
When the (A) sun be- (E7) gins to (A) shine.

A

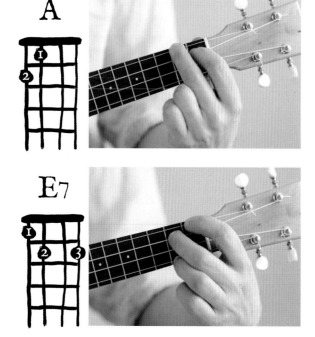

D

E7

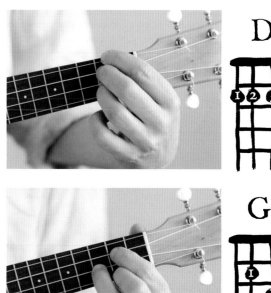

G

WHEN THE SAINTS GO MARCHING IN

2 3 4	1	2	3	4	1	2	3	4
Oh when the	saints					go	mar-	ching
	A	-	-	-	A	-	-	-
	in					Oh	when	the
	A	-	-	-	A	-	-	-
	saints		go		mar-		ching	
	A	-	-	-	A	-	-	-
	in					I	want	to
	E7	-	-	-	E7	-	-	-
	be				in		that	
	A	-	-	-	A	-	-	-
	num-	ber					When	the
	D	-	-	-	D	-	-	-
	saints		go		march-		ing	
	A	-	-	-	E7	-	-	-
	in							
	A	-	-	-	A	-	-	-

☛ You'll find that lots of other songs work over this chord progression, from 'Sloop John B' to 'She'll Be Coming Round the Mountain'. If this song is a bit high (or low) for you to sing, why not try it in a different key (see page 144)?

You could try changing all the A chords for C chords, the E7s for G7s and the Ds for Fs. Now it's the same song but in a new key, and the first notes to sing will be C, E, F for 'Oh when the...'.

MIDNIGHT SPECIAL

A favourite old tune of mine is 'Midnight Special', which I first heard performed by Huddie William 'Lead Belly' Ledbetter, and later when Creedence Clearwater Revival had a hit with it in 1969. It's a traditional folk song that is thought to have originated among prisoners in the American south. Indeed, Lead Belly's first recording of the song was made in the 'Alcatraz of the South', Louisiana State Penitentiary, where he was serving time for murder.

Our hero in this song is a train, whose light seems to signal a way out of the prison walls inside which the singer is trapped. Many artists, including The Beatles, Harry Belafonte and even ABBA have had a crack at this tune, so it's time you did too.

Take this tune nice and easy...You should be able to play along with the Creedence Clearwater version with the chords opposite. The first note to sing is an F# for 'You get up...'.

MIDNIGHT SPECIAL

You get up in the (G) morning, when that big bell (D) rings,
You go marching to the (A) table, you see the same old (D) thing,
Knife and fork are on the (G) table, but nothing in my (D) pan,
And if you say anything a- (A) bout it, you'll have trouble with the (D) man.

CHORUS
Let the Midnight (G) Special shine her light on (D) me,
Let the Midnight (A) Special, shine her ever-loving light on (D) me.

REPEAT CHORUS

Yonder come little (G) Rosie, how in the world do you (D) know?
I can tell her by her (A) apron, and the dress she (D) wore,
Umbrella on her (G) shoulder, piece of paper in her (D) hand,
She goes marching to the (A) captain, she wants to free her (D) man.

REPEAT CHORUS

If you ever go to (G) Houston, you better walk (D) right,
You better not (A) stagger, you better not (D) fight,
The sheriff will (G) arrest you, the boys will bring you (D) down,
And if the jury finds you (A) guilty, you're penitentiary (D) bound.

234	1	2	3	4	1	2	3	4
You get up in the	morn-	ning				when the	big	bell
	G	-	-	-	G	-	-	-
	rings					You go	marching	to the
	D	-	-	-	D	-	-	-
	ta-	ble			you	see the	same	old
	A	-	-	-	A	-	-	-
	thing					Knife and	fork are	on the
	D	-	-	-	D	-	-	-
	ta-	ble			but	nothing	in	my
	G	-	-	-	G	-	-	-
	pan				And if	you say	any	thing a-
	D	-	-	-	D	-	-	-
	bout	it				you'll have	trouble	with the
	A	-	-	-	A	-	-	-
	man					Let the	Midnight	
	D	-	-	-	D	-	-	-
	Spec-	ial				shine her	light on	
	G	-	-	-	G	-	-	-
	me					Let the	Midnight	
	D	-	-	-	D	-	-	-
	Spec-	ial				shine her	ever-	loving
	A	-	-	-	A	-	-	-
	light on		me						
	A	-	D	-	D	-	-	-

So far so good! Hopefully you're beginning to get comfortable with your new wooden friend and have stumbled upon a few techniques and methods of your own.

Next we'll look at some different ways to strum your ukulele, and take in a bunch of new chords that'll richen the sound you're already making. Keep writing in the chord shapes as we go and they'll stick in your head better. And listen to the songs online if you're having any problems - just visit www.willgrovewhite.com and click the *Get Plucky* button.

IT'S STRUMMERTIME!

SIMPLE STRUMMING PATTERNS

Now you're mastering a few chords, you can begin to get going on what many would argue is the real meat of ukulele playing - strumming. There are a million and one different ways to strum a ukulele and, by developing a good technique, you can transform a few simple chords into something that sounds really great.

In the songs you've just had a go at there were two basic ways you'll have been playing: straight fours (like in 'London Bridge Is Falling Down') and swung fours (like in 'When the Saints Go Marching In'). You'll probably have done these without thinking about it, but let me explain the difference.

Straight fours are when the down and the up stroke are evenly spaced, like this:

1	2	3	4
DOWN UP	DOWN UP	DOWN UP	DOWN UP

This feel is used in a lot of rock songs, like the Sex Pistols' 'God Save the Queen' and Status Quo's 'Rockin' All Over the World'. Of course, they had electric guitars, overdrive pedals and stacks of amps to play with, so the effect won't be quite that, but hey, it's a uke: what did you expect?

Swung fours have a skip to them, making the rhythm swingy, as in 'Singin' in the Rain' and other jazzy songs.

1	2	3	4
DOWN UP	DOWN UP	DOWN UP	DOWN UP

At this stage, I'd recommend concentrating on simple strumming patterns, and remember that when you're playing a song, you don't have to strum all the time. It can sound very effective if you leave a few gaps in your strums, as long as the pulse of the song isn't interrupted.

DOWNSTROKES

To go for a really heavy rock feel, try playing all downstrokes, but putting the emphasis on beats 2 and 4, like this:

1	2	3	4
DOWN	DOWN	DOWN	DOWN

OFF-BEATS

For a reggae, ska or country feel, either mute the strings (by resting your left-hand fingers across the strings - see page 146) or just don't play at all on the 1 and 3 beats, and play a crisp chord only on the 2 and 4 beats. Keeping things simple will make your playing sound more complicated!

1	2	3	4
Shh...	DOWN ↘	Shh...	DOWN ↘

WALTZ

I should also mention a waltz. This is a tune that only has 3 beats per bar, so we count 1, 2, 3, 1, 2, 3, 1, 2, 3, with the emphasis on the 1 beat. Some famous pop songs in waltz time are 'The House of the Rising Sun,' made famous by The Animals, 'Norwegian Wood' by The Beatles and 'Manic Depression' by Jimi Hendrix. A waltz can be played as one downstroke and two upstrokes, to get that boom-cha-cha-boom-cha-cha-boom-cha-cha feel. This is roughly how you do it:

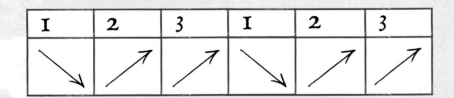

1	2	3	1	2	3
↘	↗	↗	↘	↗	↗

The different ways to strum a ukulele quickly become endless and there are masses of great tutorials on YouTube and other websites that give greater detail about more complicated strum patterns. Even a C, F and G7 chord progression can sound pretty fancy if you practise your strumming - players like George Formby used strumming to great effect, while not doing anything particularly fancy with their left hand. You can learn how to play a triple stroke on page 148, but wait a bit for that.

ROLL STROKE

One strum that you can have a go at right away (if you're feeling daring) is a roll stroke. This isn't a pattern, but a method of strumming a chord that will add texture to your playing. Rather than one finger strumming down across the strings, all four fingers roll out across them, creating a *prrrriiinnng* effect.

To try it, make your strumming hand into relaxed fist and uncurl the tips of your fingers across the strings, from top to bottom. Start with your little finger, followed by your ring, middle, and forefingers. *Prrriiinnng!* Mmm-mm.

SAD CHORDS – MINORS

This chord is easiest to play with your middle finger, like this:

Now let's learn a minor chord. A minor chord has its second note down a semitone, which has the effect of making it seem a bit more mournful than a major chord. This one is a doddle to play, and it's called A minor (see right).

Be careful not to fall into a dark depression when you play this chord. Gosh, it's sad...

A

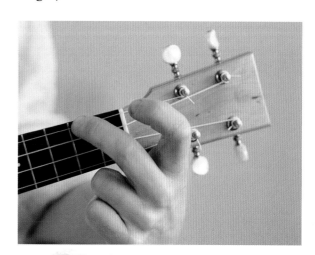

WHAT SHALL WE DO WITH A DRUNKEN SAILOR?

1	2	3	4	1	2	3	4
What	shall we	do	with a	drun-	ken	sail-	or?
Am	-	-	-	Am	-	-	-
What	shall we	do	with a	drun-	ken	sail-	or
Am	-	-	-	Am	-	-	-
Hoo-		ray	and	up	she	ri-	ses
Am	-	-	-	Am	-	-	-
Hoo-		ray	and	up	she	ri-	ses
Am	-	-	-	Am	-	-	-

Minor chords are incredibly useful, so it's worth learning a few. They'll allow you to play more complex tunes with richer structures. Some of these tunes are coming up but let's get started on an easy one. By adding this A minor chord to a G chord, we can have a go at another tune, although it's not particularly sad (apart from for the sailor once he wakes up). It's an old sea shanty, me hearties - 'What Shall We Do with a Drunken Sailor?'. I remember the Two Ronnies doing a version of this: I think it went, 'Hoorah, and up she rises / She's got ears of different sizes / One's very small and the other wins prizes / Early in the morning.'

The first note to sing is an E for 'What…'.

WHAT SHALL WE DO WITH A DRUNKEN SAILOR?

(Am) What shall we do with a drunken sailor?
(G) What shall we do with a drunken sailor?
(Am) What shall we do with a drunken sailor?
(G) Early in the (Am) morning!

YOU CAN MAKE UP YOUR OWN VERSES,
OR TRY THESE FOR SIZE:

Chuck him in the long boat 'til he's sober (×3)
(G) Early in the (Am) morning!

Give him a hair of the dog that bit him (×3)
(G) Early in the (Am) morning!

Shave his belly with a rusty razor (×3)
(G) Early in the (Am) morning!

→ 1	2	3	4	1	2	3	4
What	shall we	do	with a	drun-	ken	sail-	or?
G	-	-	-	G	-	-	-
Ear-	ly	in	the	morn-		ing	
G	-	-	-	Am	-	-	-
Hoo-		ray	and	up	she	ri-	ses
G	-	-	-	G	-	-	-
Ear-	ly	in	the	morn-		ing	
G	-	-	-	Am	-	-	-

Not many people know that 'Scarborough Fair' wasn't written by Paul Simon, but is in fact an old English folk song. Folk legend Martin Carthy transcribed the tune for Paul Simon when he met him in London, and the song went on to become the inspiration for Simon and Garfunkel's hit 1966 album, *Parsley, Sage, Rosemary and Thyme*. After the song was featured in 'The Graduate', it became a huge hit, although I prefer to remember the time that Paul Simon performed it on 'The Muppet Show'.

The first note to sing is an A for 'Are...'.

SCARBOROUGH FAIR

(Am) Are you going to (G) Scarborough (Am) Fair?
(C) Parsley, (Am) sage, rose- (D) mary, and (Am) thyme,
Remember (C) me to one who lives (G) there,
(Am) She once (G) was a true love of (Am) mine.

(Am) Tell her to make me a (G) cambric (Am) shirt,
(C) Parsley, (Am) sage, rose (D) mary, and (Am) thyme,
Without no (C) seams nor needle (G) work,
(Am) Then she'll (G) be a true love of (Am) mine.

SCARBOROUGH FAIR

1	2	3	1	2	3	1	2	3	1	2	3
Are		you	going		to	Scar-	-bor-	ough	Fair?		
Am	-	-	Am	-	-	G	-	-	Am	-	-
			Par-	sley	sage		rose-	ma-	ry	and	
Am	-	-	C	-	-	Am	-	-	D	-	-
thyme											Re-
Am	-	-	Am	-	-	Am	-	-	Am	-	-
mem-		ber	me		to	one	who	lives	there		
Am	-	-	C	-	-	C	-	-	G	-	-
			She		once	was		a	true	love	of
G	-	-	Am	-	-	G	-	-	G	-	-
mine											
Am	-	-	Am	-	-	Am	-	-	Am	-	-

MORE CHORDS PLEASE

BARRE CHORDS

Barre chords can be a bit tricky at first but they are very useful. So far you've learned quite a few chords but in each chord there have been one or two (or even three) open strings. An open string is one that isn't being fretted by one of your left-hand fingers.

Barre chords are those that need all four of the strings to be pressed down onto the fretboard, sometimes using one finger to press down two or more strings. On the right are some examples of what barre chord boxes can look like.

With the B♭ chord, you need to press the E and A strings down with your first finger, and use your second and third fingers to complete the chord.

With the D7 and C minor chords, you can see that although all four strings are being pressed down, you only need to use two fingers to play them, so you may find these tricky at first. Barre chords require you to apply more pressure with your first finger than usual, in order to press down the notes so that they ring out properly.

If it doesn't sound great at first, never fear. Keep practising and your fingers will become stronger. Remember to keep the pressure even across your finger and try to keep the finger flat so that each string produces a clear note.

See page 151 for more interesting facts about barre chords, and don't forget to take lots of breaks and eat lots of biscuits.

B♭
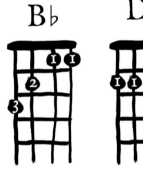

D7
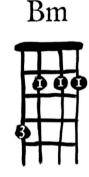

Bm
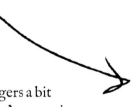

Once you've given your fingers a bit of a stretch and you feel they're up to it, here's how you might play each of them:

A very easy tune to try, which includes a barre chord, is 'St James Infirmary Blues,' a song that my grandfather used to play for me on the piano (but probably better known to you in the versions by Cab Calloway or Louis Armstrong, or in the recent cover by the White Stripes).

There are two new chords to get to grips with for this tune, F minor and C#7 (this is a D7 chord down one fret). The chord boxes look like those shown below.

And you play them like this:

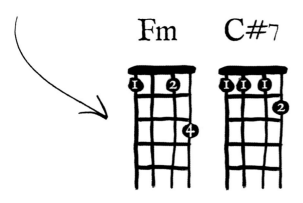

Fm   C#7

ST JAMES INFIRMARY BLUES

4	1	2	3	4	1	2	3	4 —
I went	down	to	St James	In-	firmary			
	Fm	-	C7	-	Fm	-	-	-
	stretched out	on a	long	white	table			So
	Fm	-	C7	-	Fm	-	-	-
	go	let her	go	God	bless her			
	Fm	-	C7	-	Fm	-	-	-
	search	this	wide	world	over			But she'll
	Fm	-	C7	-	Fm	-	-	-

St James Infirmary Blues

I (Fm) went down to (C₇) St. James In- (Fm) firmary,
To see my (C#₇) baby (C₇) there,
She was (Fm) stretched out on a (C₇) long, white (Fm) table,
So (C#₇) sweet, so (C₇) cold, so (Fm) fair.

Let her (Fm) go, let her (C₇) go, God (Fm) bless her,
Wherever (C#₇) she may (C₇) be,
She can (Fm) search this wide (C₇) world (Fm) over,
But she'll (C#₇) never find an- (C₇) other sweet man like (Fm) me.

Now, (Fm) when I die, (C₇) bury me in my straight-leg (Fm) britches,
Put on a box-back coat (C#₇) and a stetson (C₇) hat,
Put a (Fm) gold piece (C₇) on my (Fm) watch chain,
So all the (C#₇) boys will know I (C₇) died standing (Fm) pat.

Get six (Fm) gamblers to (C₇) carry my (Fm) coffin,
Six chorus girls (C#₇) to sing my (C₇) song,
Put a (Fm) jazz band (C₇) on my (Fm) tailgate,
To raise (C#₇) hell as we (C₇) roll (Fm) along.

The first notes to sing are F, G#, C for 'I went down…'.

→ 1	2	3	4	1	2	3	4
To see	my	ba-	by	there			She was
Fm	-	C#₇	-	C₇	-	-	-
sweet	so	cold	so	fair			Let her
C#₇	-	C₇	-	Fm	-	-	-
Where-	ever	she	may	be			She can
Fm	-	C#₇	-	C₇	-	-	-
never find		another sweet	man like	me			
C#₇	-	C₇	-	Fm	-	-	-

MORE COMMON CHORDS

Here are some more common chords for you to begin getting your sausage fingers around.

A7

B♭m

B

Cm

Dm

E

Em

CHORD Z

Chord Z is a great chord to know. You can play it at any time, in any piece of music, and it always sounds good.

All you have to do is rest your fingers gently across the strings so they are touching them but not pushing them onto the fretboard. Then strum. It should make a 'chuck' noise - no notes should sound.

The ukulele is a brilliant rhythm instrument, as we have already seen. Chord Z takes this to the extreme and turns the ukulele into a pure percussion instrument.

Often a tune needs a good, strong backbeat, and chord Z is just the ticket. Or you might want to imitate the ticking of a hi-hat - chord Z. Perhaps most importantly, it's also a great chord to play if you've completely lost your place in the music and have no idea what to do - chord Z always fits, and you'll always look like you know what you're doing.

It can also add great variety into a song. If you've got a tune with, say, three verses and three choruses, you could think about trying the third verse with just chord Z, as if the instruments have dropped out and only the drums are playing. Then, when you get to the chorus again and strum out your chords, the impact will be all the greater.

INDULGE ME

A CLASSIC TUNE

In my mind, a ukulele lesson wouldn't be complete without being able to play this classic tune. It's 'They're Red Hot' by Robert Johnson, the man who sold his soul to the devil at the crossroads. The Red Hot Chili Peppers covered this tune on their album *Blood Sugar Sex Magik*, and the Ukulele Orchestra of Great Britain have popularized it on the ukulele as 'Hot Tamales'.

The new chords are shown here.

THEY'RE RED HOT

(C) Hot ta- (E7) males and they're (A7) red hot,
(D7) Yeah she (G7) got 'em for (C) sale,
Hot ta- (E7) males and they're (A7) red hot,
(D7) Yeah she got 'em for (G7) sale,
(C) I got a girl say she's (C7) long and tall,
She (F) sleeps in the kitchen with her (D7) feets in the hall,
(C) Hot ta- (E7) males and they're (A7) red hot,
(D7) Yeah she (G7) got 'em for (C) sale I (A7) said,
(D7) Yeah she (G7) got 'em for (C) sale.

ALTERNATIVE MIDDLE LINE:
(C) Me and my girl got a (C7) V-8 Ford,
(F) We run that thing on the (D7) washing board.

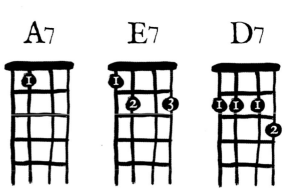

THEY'RE RED HOT

1	2	3	4	1	2	3	4
	Hot ta-	males	and they're	red	hot		
C	-	E_7	-	A_7	-	-	-
Yeah	she	got 'em	for	sale			
D_7	-	G_7	-	C	-	-	-
	Hot ta-	males	and they're	red	hot		
C	-	E_7	-	A_7	-	-	-
Yeah	she	got 'em	for	sale			
D_7	-	-	-	G_7	-	-	-
I	got a	girl	say she's	long	and	tall	She
C	-	-	-	C_7	-	-	-
sleeps	in the	kitchen	with her	feets	in the	hall	
F	-	-	-	D_7	-	-	-
	Hot ta-	males	and they're	red	hot		
C	-	E_7	-	A_7	-	-	-
Yeah	she	got 'em	for	sale	I	said	
D_7	-	G_7	-	C	-	A_7	-
Yeah	she	got 'em	for	sale			
D_7	-	G_7	-	C	-	-	-

The first note to sing is a C for 'Hot...'.

AN OLD FAVOURITE

In 1964, 'The House of the Rising Sun' was a massive hit across the globe for Newcastle band The Animals and is now recognized as one of the classics of British pop music. But by the time the band made it a success, it had already been recorded by Nina Simone, Woody Guthrie and Lead Belly, to name but a few artists. (When Bob Dylan heard The Animals' version of it on the radio he loved it, but quickly dropped it from his set list when he was accused of copying The Animals - he'd already been playing it for years.)

Wherever it came from, 'The House of the Rising Sun' is a folk song, and a cracking one at that. The earliest recordings are by Appalachian folk singers but the song's history goes back even further. It's thought to derive from the English tradition of broadside ballads like 'The Unfortunate Rake,' and it somehow made its way over to a New Orleans setting.

The first note to sing is an A for 'There is...'. Have a go and see how you get along.

COMING UP

Now that you've got this far, you may have more than enough to be getting on with. If you're feeling at all unsure, go back and pluck away at some of the first tunes again - you'll find you've already got better.

For those who want to find out more, and delve into deeper ukulele matters, we're next going to look at some simple musical theory, and at techniques that will add variety and texture to your playing, from learning how to mute the strings to blistering strums like the Triple Stroke.

HOUSE OF THE RISING SUN

There (Am) is a (C) house in (D) New Or- (F) leans,
They (Am) call the (C) Rising (E7) Sun,
It's (Am) been the (C) ruin of (D) many a poor (F) girl,
And (Am) God I (E7) know I'm (Am) one (E7).

My (Am) mother (C) was a (D) tailor (F),
She (Am) sewed those (C) new blue (E7) jeans,
My (Am) sweetheart (C) was a (D) drunkard, (F) Lord,
(Am) Down in (E7) New Or- (Am) leans (E7).

Now the (Am) only (C) thing a (D) drunkard (F) needs,
Is a (Am) suitcase (C) and a (E7) trunk,
And the (Am) only (C) time he's (D) satis- (F) fied,
Is (Am) when he's (E7) on a (Am) drunk (E7).

Go (Am) tell my (C) baby (D) sister (F),
Not to (Am) do what (C) I have (E7) done,
To (Am) shun that (C) house in (D) New Or- (F) leans,
They (Am) call the (E7) Rising (Am) Sun (E7).

Well, I got (Am) one foot (C) on the (D) platform (F),
The (Am) other foot (C) on the (E7) train,
I'm (Am) going (C) back to (D) New Or- (F) leans,
To (Am) wear that (E7) ball and (Am) chain.

HOUSE OF THE RISING SUN

3	I	2	3	I	2	3	I	2	3
There	is		a	house		in	New		Or-
	Am	-	-	**C**	-	-	**D**	-	-
	leans		They	call		the	ri-		sing
	F	-	-	**Am**	-	-	**C**	-	-
	sun					It's	been		the
	E$_7$	-	-	**E**$_7$	-	-	**Am**	-	-
	ruin		of	many		a	poor	girl	And
	C	-	-	**D**	-	-	**F**	-	-
	God		I	know		I'm	one		
	Am	-	-	**E**$_7$	-	-	**Am**	-	-

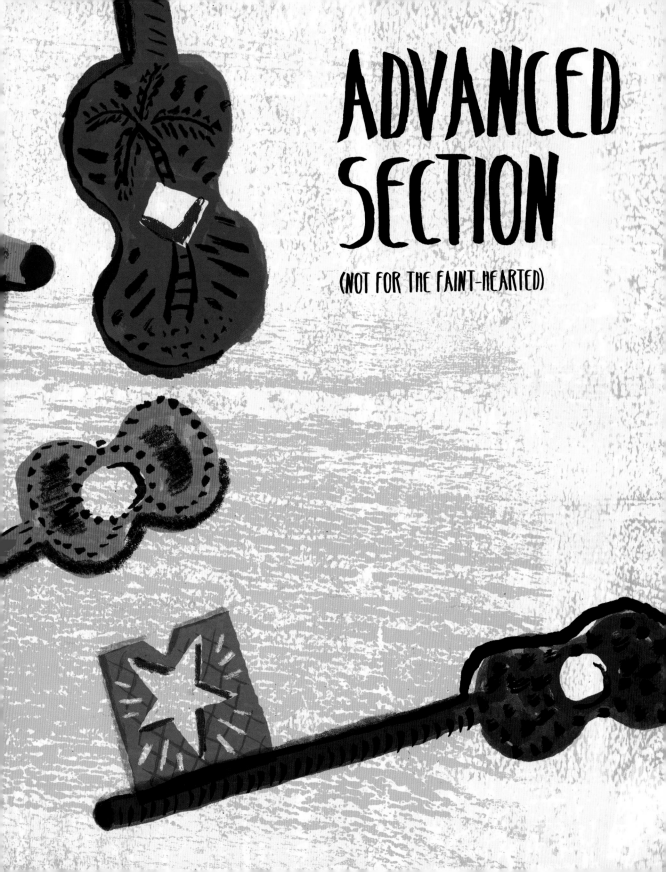

ADVANCED SECTION

(NOT FOR THE FAINT-HEARTED)

A BIT OF THEORY

DIFFERENT KEYS AND WHAT THEY ARE

Musical keys are a complex business, with majors and minors, modulations and tonics ('I'd like a large modulation and tonic, barman'). For our purposes, and in much of popular music, the key is the main note and chord of a piece, the one that often begins and resolves it.

To explain what different keys are, I'm going to ask you to sing 'Twinkle Twinkle Little Star'. Okay? Done that? It sounded lovely. Now sing it again but start singing 'Twinkle' on the same note on which you sang 'star'. You'll find that the whole song becomes higher. Even though it's the same tune, and we all recognize it as 'Twinkle Twinkle Little Star', all the notes have now changed. That's because you're now singing it in a different *key* from the one that you started in.

If you've got a song and the chords, but you're finding it too high (or low) to sing properly, you'll need to change the key that the song is in. This means moving every chord down (or up) by a certain number of semitones.

If you look at the diagram below, which shows all 12 notes in the musical scale, you can figure out how to make a song higher or lower. Let's say, for example, that we're trying to play a piece in C, which has the chords C, F and G in it, but it's too high to sing and we want to make it lower.

Let's try moving it down five semitones, so that it begins in G instead - we're turning what was the C chord into a G chord. Now we do the same thing to the other chords - move the F and G down five semitones, and turn them into C and D. Now we just substitute the old chords for the new ones and off we go. You've moved the song into a lower key and it should be easier for you to sing.

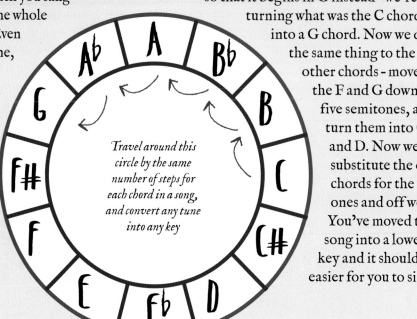

Travel around this circle by the same number of steps for each chord in a song, and convert any tune into any key

PICKING AND STRUMMING VARIATIONS

FINGERPICKING

A nice way to add interest to your ukulele playing is to do some fingerpicking. This means plucking the separate strings of a chord in a rhythm. The beauty of fingerpicking is that it can sound quite fancy without your left hand having to do much. It just sits there holding the chord shape while the right hand picks out the notes.

There are a thousand different ways to fingerpick, but a good starting point is to try plucking the top three strings (the C, E and A) in this pattern:

A-E-C / A-E-C / A-E-C / A-E-C

Start by using your middle finger (3) to pluck the A string, your forefinger (2) for the E string, and your thumb (1) for the C string. Once you've got this rolling along, you can add in some different chord shapes with your left hand:

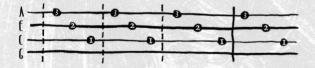

Another simple pattern is to alternate between the C and G strings with your thumb on the 1, 2, 3, 4 beats and then pluck both the E and A strings at the same time with your first and middle fingers on the 'and' beats, like this:

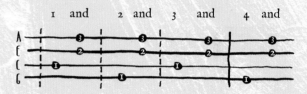

The next pattern will get more fingers moving. Starting with your thumb on the G string, pluck up and down the four strings with each finger (apart from your little finger), then pluck back down again. It's called an arpeggio. Fancy, huh?

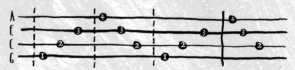

Once you're fluent with these patterns, you can begin experimenting with some of your own, or patterns stolen from banjo and guitar tutor books.

MUTING THE STRINGS

Another great variation on a normal strumming sound is to mute the strings. This gives a distinctive 'plunky' sound, which is great for rocky numbers or funky rhythms. I find the easiest way to do this is to rest the outer pad of my right hand across the bridge, so that it's actually touching the strings, and then strum with my forefinger. Of course, you can't move your wrist in this case so you have to strum using the base of your finger as the pivot.

This has the effect of muting the strings and producing short notes that hardly resonate at all. You should still be able to hear the notes themselves but they should have no sustain. Pure plunk heaven.

Position the pad of your hand just across the bridge. As you roll your palm onto the strings it will mute them more.

STOPPING THE STRINGS

1. *Stop the strings to get a 'clack'...*

2. *...then strum so the notes ring out.*

With just one or two chords and some clever strumming, you can get some great rhythmical effects. One technique I use is to stop the strings with the spare fingers on my left hand (the ones that aren't forming a chord) while strumming. This way you can create a variety of sounds just by moving your fingers on and off the strings.

First, position your left hand so it's playing a C chord. For the first beat, lightly rest your first and second fingers across the other three strings while you gently raise your third finger off the A string (so it's just resting on it). Now strum. It won't sound a chord because all the strings are being muted by your fingers but it will create a 'clack' sound. This is the idea.

For the second beat, lift your first and second fingers off the strings, push your third finger down onto the third fret of the A string and strum again. This time the C chord will sound. Now repeat the whole process. The effect you're after is: clack-chord-clack-chord-clack-chord.

By resting your fingers back on the strings after you've played the chord, it will stop the notes, making the sound nice and punchy.

Once you've mastered this simple technique, you can apply it to other chords. In the case of D7 you can simply raise your left-hand fingers half off the fretboard, which will create the 'clack' and stop the notes, then push them back down to create the chord.

Using your left-hand fingers to stop the strings sounding will quickly lead you to discover new and interesting rhythms that can make your playing richer and more varied, from clack-chord-clack-chord to clacker-clacker-chord-a-chord-a. Did that make any sense? I'm just trying to encourage you to embrace the percussive nature of the ukulele and experiment with techniques like this to do so. There is much more to ukulele strumming than a simple up-and-down, up-and-down rhythm.

A TRIPLE STROKE

This sounds like either a life-threatening condition or a complicated petting procedure. It is, in fact, a nifty strum that will add pizzazz to any tune, make you more attractive, hoover behind the sofa and take the dog for a walk.

The triple stroke was widely used in the 1920s and 1930s by artists like Cliff Edwards (see pages 20-1) and Roy Smeck, and then by George Formby (see pages 24-7) and Tessie O'Shea (see page 31) on their banjo-ukuleles in the 1940s. It's a clever move because it turns one strumming movement into three strummed chords.

To play it, all you need to do is introduce your right thumb into a normal strum. Form your right forefinger and thumb into a 'C' shape. Keeping this 'C' shape, strum the strings with your forefinger (see fig. 1) and then follow through with another strum from the pad of your thumb (see fig. 2). This is the key move - you're adding a strum into a pattern where there wasn't one before. Once you've got this far, you come back up the strings with the pad of your forefinger, forming a complete 'dig-ger-di' (see fig. 3).

Now have a go at turning a four-beat strum - down-down-down-down - into down-down-downdownup-down. I've used a syllable for each strum here. The rhythm you're aiming for is: dum-dum-diggerdi-dum.

Some methodical practice of this move will eventually bring you joy but not before you've cursed my name a thousand times. It adds a lazy triple to any strum and adds a certain *joie de vivre* to even the simplest of tunes. First, perfect it at a slow tempo, then gradually up the speed until you're strumming like a wild banshee. If this still isn't clear, look on YouTube, where it has been carefully explained by an array of ukulele maestros, and you can see and hear it in action.

1. *Forefinger strums down...*

2. *...followed by the thumb...*

3. *...and back up again with the first.*

PLAYING TUNES ON THE UKULELE

The ukulele is a wonderful melody instrument - all the notes from middle C to a high A are there for you to pluck, so for those with some knowledge of written music or just an ear for a tune, below is a neat diagram of where all the notes are on your ukulele fretboard. Any of you who know a few guitar riffs or licks can easily transfer them directly to the ukulele - remember, the relationship between the highest four strings on a guitar is the same as on a ukulele so, although the key might be different, the patterns will fit.

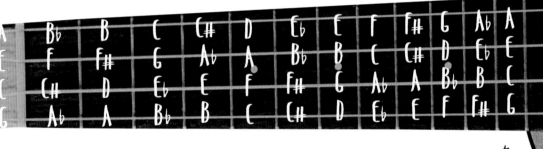

5TH FRET   12TH FRET

Another satisfying way to play melodies on your ukulele is to pick out the notes from the chord shapes that you are forming. Very often you'll find that the chord you're playing contains one or more of the notes in the melody of the song.

For most melody plucking, though, it's down to the nitty-gritty of listening to a tune and then hunting around on the fretboard for the simplest way to play it. (And when it comes to plucking a solo, often just a few different notes will do. Find three or four that sound good and have a play around with them.)

Remember, there's more than one way to play nearly every note on the ukulele, so search around until you find the most straightforward pattern for the tune - try not to end up playing the whole melody on one string, zooming up and down the fretboard like a madman.

TABS – WHAT THEY ARE AND HOW TO READ THEM

I said I wouldn't give you any musical notation, and I won't, but it would be churlish of me not to explain how to read ukulele tablature, or 'tabs'. I'm only doing this so those of you who want to venture forth into the world of the internet and all the ukulele goodies that await you there will know what tabs are and how you can read them.

Tablature is a way of writing out a tune without having to resort to traditional musical notation. The four horizontal lines represent the strings of the ukulele, as if looking down at them from a player's point of view, so the top line of the tablature refers to the A string, and the bottom line is the G string:

UKE NECK

This is what an F chord looks like when written out in tab form:

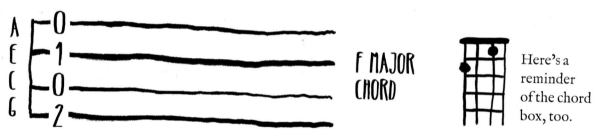

F MAJOR CHORD

Here's a reminder of the chord box, too.

The numbers show which fret to put your finger on to get the right note. So the 1 on the second line down means you play the first fret of the E string. The 2 on the bottom line means you play the second fret of the G string.

When it comes to written tunes, there will be a time signature (4/4 if there are 4 beats in the bar, 3/4 if there are 3) and bar lines marked out. There's also a rhythmical notation system

– a series of dots and dashes – that lets you know how long to hold each note for, but I won't go into that here for fear of information overload! If you want more advice on ukulele tabs and how to read them, I recommend visiting ukulele tab websites, of which there are many.

We'll leave tabs with this tune for you to have a go at: 'Twinkle Twinkle Little Star'. Start with two notes on the open C string:

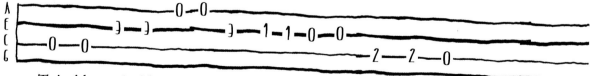

Twin-kle, twin-kle, Lit-tle star. How I won-der what you are

INVERSIONS

So far we've concentrated on the first few frets of the ukulele. So what's the rest of it for? The higher frets, or 'the dusty end' as it's sometimes known, are often used to play tunes on, but can also be utilized to play higher versions of the chords you already know.

An 'inversion' of a chord is the same chord but played using a different shape. As you'll usually be moving up the neck to play inversions, they are all barre chords (see box, below), so only have a go at these once your fingers have built up a bit of strength. Inversions are great alternatives to first-position chords, because they create different-sounding chords, which add variety and interest to your strumming.

Below are some examples of inversions of chords you already know. They are the same chords, but played in a different position.

C MAJOR INVERSIONS

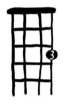 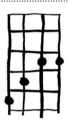 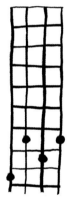

Have a go playing C major in first, second and third positions.

A7 INVERSIONS

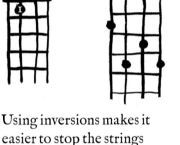  

Using inversions makes it easier to stop the strings (see page 147).

THE BARRE NECESSITIES

When you play a barre chord the finger that's stretched across the fretboard acts as a 'movable nut'

C_7 $C\#_7$ D_7

  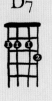

(the nut is the hard strip that the strings run through between the fretboard and the tuning pegs).

Look at the D_7 chord shape while thinking about the C_7 chord shape you learned for 'Baby Please Don't Go' (see pages 110-11). In the C_7 shape, the ukulele nut is doing the same job as your first finger in the D_7 chord shape. If we move a C_7 chord up two frets, it becomes a D_7 chord. This is because each time we move one fret up the neck of a uke, the note moves up one semitone, and D is two semitones above C. In the same way, if we move the D_7 shape two frets further up the fretboard, it becomes an E_7.

This is why barre chords are so handy - they are MOVABLE.

TUNE YOUR UKE DIFFERENTLY

Having given you all this information about how to play the ukulele, I'm now going to encourage you to have a go at tuning your ukulele differently. Convention dictates that one should stick to the set, historically approved tuning for certain instruments, but a ukulele is a four-stringed instrument that can be tuned up in any way, so why not have a go? No one's going to rap your knuckles. It's very common for guitarists to retune their guitars to give themselves some different options, so why shouldn't ukulelists do the same?

LOW G VS HIGH G

Those of you who, like me, think the ukulele sounds good tuned with the eccentric higher G string (nearest your nose) can skip this bit. I know there are some of you out there, though, who can't abide the sheer chirpiness of this little instrument and would like a bit more 'bottom end' (lower notes) on your ukulele. This is entirely possible. Some people prefer to tune their ukuleles with a low G string, an octave below the normal tuning, to give more depth to the sound. This can be very nice if you're planning on playing a lot of solo performances, where the intense shrillness of a normally tuned uke is felt by some to be a little grating.

In this case, simply get your hands on some soprano ukulele strings with a 'low G' and then follow the instructions for changing your strings and tuning as normal (see pages 166–7). All the chord shapes are the same; you will just have one string that is an octave lower than on a normal uke.

ADF#B

Sometimes known as the 'English' ukulele tuning, this was actually popularized by the American ukulele revolutionary May Singhi Breen (see page 33). ADF#B is the same relative tuning as GCEA but a tone higher. This has the knock-on effect of making all the chord names different but it can sound great when combined with GCEA-tuned ukuleles because the voicings of each chord are altered, adding a tonal variety that would otherwise be lacking.

GCEG

One easy thing you can try is to tune your ukulele to an open major chord. The easiest way to do this is to tune it to GCEG - this is the same as a bluegrass banjo without the drone string. All you have to do is change the A note on the top string to a G note by loosening it a bit. Once it's in tune you'll be able to hear that it's tuned to a major chord - a C. Now a single finger across all four strings will create a major barre chord, so you can play all sorts of songs with just one finger. You can try a one-finger version of '(Sittin' On) The Dock of the Bay' by starting the song on the open chord then moving up to a barre on the 4th fret on the word 'sun'. Then up to the 5th fret for 'sitting', and then slide down a fret for each syllable of 'evening comes'.

This GCEG banjo tuning is also favoured by Keith Richards of The Rolling Stones. Mr Richards has been playing a five-string guitar for most of his career (tuned GDGBD), proving that even rock-star guitarists feel the draw of fewer strings. As we only have four strings, we lose the bottom G string and move the tuning up by three tones, making it GCEG.

A really fun thing to try now is to strum the open strings while adding and removing the note on the first fret of the E string. Cue instant Rolling Stones! Now have a go at making a new barre chord on the third fret with your first finger and adding in the extra note (a fret above the barre on the E string) with your second finger. Keep on strumming! The next thing to do is to move this shape up another fret, still taking your finger on and off the extra note on the E string - everything now sounds like the Stones.

GDAE

Why stop there? You can even tune a ukulele up like a violin or mandolin - to GDAE. You'll need to get a wound metal string for the low G and use a very thin nylon string for the high top note, but then you'll have a ukulele tuned like a violin, which makes it perfect for picking out a tune. If you can read music for violin, even better! Soon you'll be doing Mozart string quartets on the ukulele.

DIFFERENT OCTAVES

A final idea is to re-string your ukulele with, off the top of my head, a low G, but a high C and E and a low A. All your chord shapes will be the same, but the voicings of the chords will be different and this will lead you to try new and surprising things. The key is to experiment. Don't let tradition dictate what you should or shouldn't do with your ukulele. It's meant to be fun, so have a go, try something new, and soon you'll be having a whale of a time.

FIND MORE MUSIC

Given the tools you now have at your fingertips, you can start to write your own songs, or play other people's. In any music shop and on the internet you can find heaps of sheet music. Nearly all notated music has the chord names written above the lyrics, and now that you have our handy pull-out ukulele chord dictionary at the back of this book, you can simply draw in the ukulele chord boxes on the music and play along with any song you like.

A quick word of warning, though, about searching for music online. If you search for, let's say, 'Ziggy Stardust chords,' you'll find a lot of sites with the lyrics and chords to 'Ziggy Stardust'. Now, it may be that they're the right chords, but then again, it may be that they're not. Chords and lyrics are posted by users around the world and can vary greatly in their accuracy. If they sound wrong, it may well be because they *are* wrong, not because you're playing them badly.

I find that it's often best to use these sites as a starting point for figuring out the chords to a song. Once I've had a go at some chords pulled off the internet, I put on the tune and compare. The trouble comes when I realize the song and the chords from the internet are completely at odds with each other. In these cases there's often no choice but to work out the tune by ear.

HOW TO WORK OUT THE CHORDS TO A SONG BY EAR

Working out the chords to a song by ear can be a frustrating business, there's no doubt about it, but there are a few good tips I can offer that should help you out.

Before you start, make sure your ukulele is in tune - this way you'll be able to properly identify the notes that you can hear - and have our pull-out chord dictionary (see the back of the book) by your side. Also make sure you use a CD player with a pause button, or a program on your computer that lets you easily pause and rewind MP3s. It'll make life a lot easier if you can scroll back and forth through the track. Trying to work out tunes by listening is great practice and will tune your ears up nicely for the future. Don't give up!

Now, take it one step at a time...

1. Listen to the track carefully and try to identify the time signature it's in and at which points the chords change. Remember, they may change a lot less than you think. You can have a lot of melody going on over just one chord.

2. An awful lot of pop music is based around only three or four chords. These are usually the three blues chords in that key (see pages 122-7), plus a minor chord to give it some depth. So if it's a pop tune, find the main chord of the song (usually the one that finishes it), then identify the fourth and fifth notes up the octave from it and see if those chords work.

3. Listen to what the bass in the song is playing. More often than not, the bass will be playing what's known as the 'root' note. If you can hear what the bass is playing then hunt out the same note on your ukulele and find out what it's called (see the diagram of notes on the fretboard on page 149 if you're unsure). That'll be a clue to the name of the chord that's being played. Now you can experiment with the different types of chord - is it a minor chord, a major chord, or perhaps a seventh? Try them out and see if one fits.

4. Some chords can be devilishly difficult to identify. The bass player might be busy noodling away somewhere up the neck, making it impossible to pick apart the jumble of tones that are left over. In this case, it's often just a process of elimination. Find one note that you're sure will be in the chord, and try out every chord you know with that note in it. There's got to be one that will work.

5. If at this point you still can't figure it out, I suggest going for a leisurely stroll followed by a quick snooze in your favourite armchair. Very often, when you come back to a problem tune after a bit of time away from it, it becomes a lot easier to figure out.

6. If things still aren't working out and you don't know anyone good at musical theory, then purchasing the sheet music is the only thing left to do, but rather than seeing this as a failure, view it as part of your learning curve. You can buy sheet music very cheaply and quickly these days on the internet, and by going through the song with the correct chords, you'll learn where you went wrong and hopefully be able to avoid making those mistakes again in future.

WRITE YOUR OWN SONGS

Ukuleles are brilliant instruments to write your own songs with, partly because they're simple instruments that won't forgive a bad tune. A song has to be pretty strong to stand up on a ukulele, and lots of well-known composers and songwriters use the ukulele as part of the writing process.

Rock journalist Keith Altham told me a story about the time he took a journey on the London Underground with songwriter Jerry Lordan. In the middle of a crowded carriage, Lordan fished a ukulele out of his bag and started plucking away on it, explaining that this was a tune of his that The Shadows were interested in. The song was 'Apache', which would go on to be The Shadows' biggest hit. Lordan wrote 'Apache' on the ukulele, just as he would write many others, favouring the uke's simplicity and portability.

Now, like Jerry Lordan, you may already be brimming with ideas for your own songs, but if not, here are a few ideas to get you started:

☞ Find a chord progression you like and use it as the basis for a song of your own. You may think this is a bit like stealing, and it is a *bit* like stealing, but most chord progressions are as old as the hills and have been used in classical or folk music for hundreds of years. David Bowie famously used the chords for 'My Way' in his song 'Life on Mars', so don't be shy. All artists steal ideas from each other. Look at it more as a good starting point for a new song. The things that really need to be original are the words and the tune.

☞ Take a song that you love and write new lyrics for it. Next, forget about the original tune and write a new one to the lyrics you've just written. You can do this the other way around, too - write a new tune to some already existing words, then remove those words and write some original ones to fit your new tune. Using this method often leads you to use rhyming schemes you might not otherwise consider, which in turn will change the way you structure a song.

☞ Write about things from your life. Songs can be about all sorts of things, from the trivial to the profound. If your life doesn't appeal, then try someone else's. Try to put yourself in another character's shoes and write about the world from their point of view. Randy Newman did this (even with characters he hated) to great effect.

☞ Write a blues song. The blues is now such a staple of music that pretty much every musician has one such song up their sleeve. There's plenty to be blue about these days, so why not put pen to paper and release some of that existential angst?

PERFORMING TIPS

Now you've got a uke, people will often say, 'Give us a tune, then.' These words may be music to your ears, in which case you can jump up and strum away to your heart's content. Or perhaps the thought of performing in front of anyone fills you with a feeling of utter dread. Although I'm happy performing on a stage, I used to be in the latter category if asked to do something at a family gathering or the like. I just wanted the ground to swallow me up.

The key thing that helped me to play at these events was to remember that if people ask you to play something, it's only because they want to hear it, and because hearing someone perform music is a terrific thing. They're not asking you because they feel they should, when secretly they don't want you to play. They are acknowledging that you have a skill, and are asking you to delight them. So go for it! Here are some more tips:

☞ If you're nervous, try playing a song that everyone can sing along to and, once the heat has gone from your cheeks, have a go at one on your own. It's always easier once you've got started. Once you've strummed through whatever it is you're going to play, you'll find that people will be delighted and say, 'That was great!' or 'You're amazing!' or even, 'Let me give you all my money!' Well, not that, but we can live in hope.

☞ The important thing to remember about getting a compliment for your playing or singing is to take it. If someone tells you something nice about your performance, take a big breath and say, 'Thanks.' It's very easy to do and makes a real difference to the way you'll feel about playing to people in the future. There's nothing worse than telling someone you loved their singing (when you genuinely did) and hearing them reply, 'Oh no, I've got a terrible voice, I was awful.' When you give a compliment to someone, you want them to take it, so when you get one yourself, grasp it with both hands.

☞ Once you're in the swing of performing, remember that people want to see you perform! Think about what you like when you see other artists perform. Is it the way they look at the audience, a particular expression or the way they leap around? Or maybe they introduce some theatrical element into their show, like costume, lights, a tiny model of Stonehenge, a touch of drama? Whatever it is, make sure you don't just stand there staring at the floor. Look up and try to engage with your audience.

☞ If you're singing, remember to sing out. It's excruciating seeing someone mumble their way through a song. The audience wants to hear you. Even if you've got a voice like a rusty door hinge, they'd rather hear it LOUD than not at all.

☞ Vary your set. Two slow ballads can be greatly improved by popping a more up-tempo tune in between them. Or try playing a mournful instrumental in between two jolly country tunes. A varied set is a treat for an audience, so spend time thinking about it before you plough through half an hour of George Formby numbers.

☞ Lastly, leave them wanting more! Otherwise they'll be wanting you to leave more.

PLAYING IN A GROUP

Don't forget, if you've just started out on the ukulele, it doesn't mean that you can only play with other ukulele players. Ukulele players often seem to stick together, but I would absolutely encourage you to branch out and play with musicians who play different instruments.

Now that you've mastered playing chords, the world of music is your oyster. Even classical music can be broken down into chords, so if you can find a willing Philharmonic Orchestra to strum alongside, you could do just that, and it would sound great. Notes are notes, no matter which instrument they're played on.

Artists like The Magnetic Fields, Cliff Edwards and Damon Albarn have all shown how the sound of a ukulele fits wonderfully with other instruments. A particular favourite band of mine are the tUnE-yArDs, fronted by the wonderful Merrill Garbus (pictured below). She uses her ukulele in innovative ways, looping it and scratching away on it while accompanied by drums, bass, saxophones and more.

Some people fancy playing melodies and doing wild solos on their ukulele, and if that's you, go for it! The uke is a great instrument to play tunes on. Don't forget, though, what a wonderful rhythm instrument it is, supporting a melody instrument. The ukulele sounds great accompanying a clarinet or a piano, a trumpet or an electric guitar - there are no limits to the possibilities now you've got a uke.

Below: Merrill Garbus would always shout fiercely at anyone who suggested her guitar had shrunk in the wash.

PLAYING IN A UKULELE-ONLY GROUP

For those of you who want your group ukulele plucking to have a bit more structure than the average pub strum-along and are aiming to get some songs together for performance, I have one basic thought to offer. The most important thing to remember is that even though you're all playing the same instrument, you don't all have to play the same thing.

A gaggle of ukuleles all strumming away can sound fine, but it'll sound so much better if you begin to arrange parts for yourselves. On its own, an individual part might seem boring or unchallenging (only playing on the first beat of the bar, for example), but put several simple parts together and it creates a unified whole that sounds better than anything one single person is playing. To grasp this, you really have to try it out.

For example, when playing a tune like 'When the Saints Go Marching In,' five ukulele players could divide up the playing like this:

1. One person strums on all four beats.
2. One person plays the 'off-beat' (this is playing a crisp, short chord on the 2 and 4 beats - chord Z could also be used for this, see page 137).
3. One plays only the first beat of the bar (a power chord).
4. Another plays the tune.
5. Another plucks a harmony to the tune.

If you can induce a bass player to join in as well, playing root notes on beats 1 and 3, it'll start sounding like a real band.

Above: A dapper Madeiran Machete and Guitar Orchestra, 1890.

SOME CHORD PROGRESSIONS TO SEE YOU ON YOUR WAY

What follows are some of my favourite chord progressions, mostly in the key of C (because it's nice and easy). They can be transposed into any key you like, though. I found that when I started playing the ukulele I sometimes just wanted to kick off my shoes and have a strum. These chord progressions are just the ticket for when you're in this kind of mood. You may find that as you strum away, you can hear a few tunes you already know that might go well with these progressions, or you may dream up a few tunes of your own. Anyhow, muck about with them, play them fast or slow, inside out or upside down.

Each box represents a bar of four beats and, if there are two chords in a box, you should play each for two beats. All these progressions can be repeated ad infinitum...well, at least until your fingers get sore!

FIRST CHORD PROGRESSION

F - - -	Am - - -	Cm - - -	D$_7$ - - -
Gm - - -	Gm$_7$ - - -	C$_7$ - - -	C$_7$ - - -

SECOND CHORD PROGRESSION

C - - -	B$_7$ - - -	C - - -	A$_7$ - - -
D$_7$ - - -	G$_7$ - - -	C - A$_7$ -	D$_7$ - G$_7$ -

THIRD CHORD PROGRESSION

F - D$_7$ -	Gm$_7$ - E$_7$ -	Am-Aaug-	B♭ - B♭m -
F - D$_7$ -	Gm$_7$ - C$_7$ -	F - D$_7$ -	Gm$_7$ - C$_7$ -

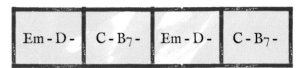

FOURTH CHORD PROGRESSION

C - Em$_7$ -	A$_7$ - - -	Dm$_7$ - - -	E♭dim - - -
C - - -	E$_7$ - - -	F - - -	A$_7$ - - -
Dm$_7$ - - -	G$_7$ - - -	C - - -	Am$_7$ - - -
D$_7$ - Am$_7$ -	D$_7$ - - -	G$_7$ - Gdim -	G$_7$ - - -
C - Em$_7$ -	A$_7$ - - -	Dm$_7$ - - -	E♭dim - - -
C - - -	E$_7$ - - -	F - - -	A$_7$ - - -
Dm$_7$ - - -	E♭dim - - -	C - B♭$_7$ -	A$_7$ - - -
D$_7$ - - -	G$_7$ - - -	C - Am$_7$ -	Dm$_7$ - G$_7$ -

SIXTH CHORD PROGRESSION

Em - D -	C - B$_7$ -	Em - D -	C - B$_7$ -

SEVENTH CHORD PROGRESSION

G - - -	Em - - -	C - - -	D - - -

EIGHTH CHORD PROGRESSION

C - A$_7$ -	Dm - G$_7$ -	C - A$_7$ -	D$_7$ - G$_7$ -
C - C$_7$ -	F - Cdim -	C - A$_7$ -	D$_7$ - G$_7$ -

FIFTH CHORD PROGRESSION

F - Dm -	Gm$_7$ - C$_7$ -	F - Dm -	Gm$_7$ - C$_7$ -
F - Dm -	Gm$_7$ - C$_7$ -	F - C$_7$ -	F - - -

NINTH CHORD PROGRESSION

Fm - - -	C#$_7$ - C$_7$ -	Fm - - -	C#$_7$ - C$_7$ -
Fm - - -	C#$_7$ - C$_7$ -	C#$_7$ - C$_7$ -	Fm - - -

TROUBLE-
SHOOTING

UKULELE HOWS AND WHYS

NOTES AREN'T SOUNDING PROPERLY, I CAN HEAR BUZZING STRINGS

Make sure you're pressing the strings down firmly, just behind the fret. If there's still a buzzing noise, or a note isn't sounding properly, turn your ukulele on its side, press the problem chord shape and check that the strings aren't hitting a fret you don't want them to. If they are, then you may need to make your bridge a little higher, or file down one of the frets. This isn't a very common problem, but can be very frustrating if it happens to you.

MY UKULELE KEEPS GOING OUT OF TUNE

Tighten the screws on the tuning pegs up, and change your strings. Also, make sure you have an electronic tuner. This will make life much easier. Don't worry! All instruments go out of tune.

MEMBERS OF THE OPPOSITE SEX ARE MAGNETICALLY ATTRACTED TO ME

Are you sure you're playing a ukulele? I think you may have an electric guitar there.

HOW DO I PLAY AN E CHORD?

The E chord can be a tricky one to play. There are, though, a few options. Either you perform a yoga move with your fingers, like so:

Or you make a barre with your forefinger on the fourth fret and add in the high E with your fourth finger.

Both of these methods can prove tricky, but after some practice, they'll become easier. (For what it's worth, I find the barre chord version easier.) But as a final option, and a good one at that, simply form the shape for a D chord, move it up two frets and don't play the top A string. Hey presto!

HOW DO I PLAY A DIMINISHED CHORD?

Diminished chords are lovely, and there's a very simple trick to knowing if you're playing the right one. The fingering for diminished chords is always the same on a uke (see below) - only the positioning of the chord shape on the fretboard varies (if you're playing it on the first fret, the open strings will be acting as your first and second fingers).

To find out if a diminished chord is, say, a C diminished, just ask the question: is there a C note in the chord? Look at the diagram showing the notes on the fretboard if you're unsure which note is which (see page 149). If the answer is yes, then it's a C diminished chord. This works for all diminished chords on the ukulele.

In the same way, a C diminished chord, which looks like this:

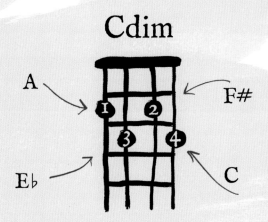

...has the notes A, E♭, F# and C in it. As a result, that chord shape is also A diminished, E♭ diminished and F# diminished, as well as C diminished. Nice, eh? In other diminished chord news, the first inversion of any of the diminished chords is the same chord shape, just up three frets. Woo-hoo!

I THINK I WANT TO BUY ANOTHER UKULELE

I've already warned you about this, but, well... go on, then.

IT'LL GET BETTER

Ukuleles sound better the more you play them - their sound mellows with age. I met a fantastic ukulele maker in America called Ron L Saul who has gone so far as to develop a ukulele-strumming machine (see below). It strums each of his handmade ukuleles over a million times before it's ready to be dispatched. A sort of pre-mellowed ukulele.

So keep playing your ukulele and it'll sound sweeter every day. Or build a crazy contraption like Ron did.

GIVING YOUR UKULELE A NEW SET OF STRINGS

A lovely thing about the ukulele is that you don't have to change your strings very often. I've met people who've been playing the same ukulele, with the same strings on, for years and years, and it still sounds great. However, there usually comes a time in a strummer's life when there's no other option but to put some fresh strings on, so you might as well be prepared for the inevitable.

First - and this is the fun bit - get some scissors and snip off the old strings, right through the middle (see picture, above right).

This is sometimes discouraged, as it can be a bit of a surprise for your ukulele, but it does feel good. Of course, if you don't want to shock your uke, just loosen and change the strings one at a time. Whichever method you choose, you can now strip off the old strings and save them for when your children need a set of whiskers for the cat mask they're making.

You should now enjoy the sight of your naked ukulele (see picture, below right). With no strings, the uke always looks very vulnerable to me, totally pointless, like an empty wine glass. It will also give you a chance to give the fretboard a bit of a clean and a dust (especially up at the top end).

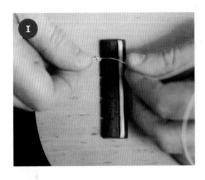

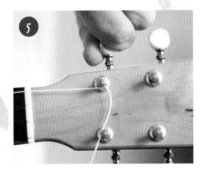

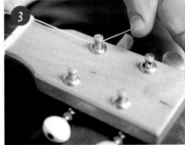

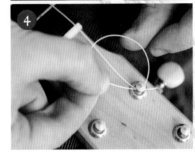

First, you'll need some new strings (see page 95). Ukulele strings can be found very easily on the internet. The next thing you need to do is tie a simple knot or two in one end of the string marked G (you can start on whichever string you want, though).

The bridge on your ukulele will probably be one of two sorts - it should either have four holes through which you thread each string, or a series of notches, inside of which each knot will stick. Either way, secure your first string to the bridge, with a good knot providing the anchor (see fig. 1), and pull it so that it's tight. Make sure the knot is big enough to stop it slipping through the hole or notch, otherwise the string will twang through when you tighten it up (some people like to use a bead above the knot to ensure this doesn't happen). Now pass the string up to its tuning peg (see fig. 2) and pass it through the hole

in the peg. Pull this so there's no slack (see fig. 3) and now pass it through the hole again, from the same side as you did before, to secure it (see fig. 4).

You don't need to leave much slack on the string across the fretboard because now you're going to start tightening it up to bring it into tune (use your electronic tuner for this bit if you have one).

Twist the tuning peg so that the string gets tighter and the note it makes gets

higher and higher. Make sure that it's winding onto the *inside* of the peg (see fig. 5). There's a huge amount of tension at this moment, and not just on the string. As the tone of the note climbs ever higher, you'll find your face twisting into a painful grimace as you envisage the string twanging in two and snapping across the back of your hand. Fear not, it'll hold.

Once you've got it roughly in tune, get to work on the other three strings.

When you're done, you'll need to play them in. New strings go out of tune for a while as they settle down. Give the uke a good strum, give the strings a vigorous tug and then retune them. Repeat this process a few times and then call it a day for a bit. When you return to your uke, it'll probably be out of tune again, but don't worry. Keep playing it and pulling the strings, and they'll settle into place. Nice. Like a new pair of socks.

AFTERWORD

PLUCKING HELL

Pitfall warnings for ukulele players, and tricks for getting round them.

Not everyone wants to hear you play your ukulele.
This is a fact, and one that some ukulele players would do well to attend to. Everyone loves a bit of music, but the most important thing is to leave your audience wanting more; don't just keep going until they've been driven mad. Ukuleles are great, but like most things, sweetest in small doses.

Beware of Hawaiian shirts.
Somehow, when people start playing the ukulele, they seem to be magnetically drawn towards short-sleeved Hawaiian-style shirts. Vividly coloured and highly patterned, these often overpowering fashion statements should be kept to a minimum.

Avoid chronic ukulele puns, such as 'uke-tastic'.
Yes, we all like a pun - there are quite a few of them in this book - but there is a growing tendency among some ukulele communities to put the word 'uke' in place of another and assume that it's a knockout bit of comedy gold. Such 'hilarious' rock 'n' roll 'puns' as 'We will Uke you!', 'Stairway to Uke-dom' and 'Bohemian Uke-sody' are just a few unforgivable crimes against the ukulele.

There's no such thing as owning just one ukulele.
I have touched on this earlier, but it can be hard to own just one ukulele. They're so small that, well, it can't hurt to get one more, can it? All I can say is, you've been warned. A lot of small things add up to a big heap of stuff, and you'll need somewhere to put them.

The ukulele has no sustain.
'Doink'. That's the noise a ukulele makes when you pluck it. 'Doink'. This can be a frustration for the ukulelist, especially when he compares the instrument to something like a keyboard, clarinet or trumpet. These instruments can make their notes last, make them sing, 'Laaaaaaaaaa!' whereas, no matter how he plucks it, the ukulele player only ever goes 'doink'.

People often ask you about George Formby.
Or it may be Tiny Tim, if you're American. Whichever ukulele player from history people talk to you about, you'll find that the non-ukulele player will be convinced that George Formby or Tiny Tim holds a special place in your heart and that you'd really like nothing more than to be that person. I notice that piano players don't get the same treatment. People don't walk up to classical pianists and say, 'Eh, I bet you're fond of Elton John!'

The ukulele is irrepressibly cheerful, and sometimes you don't want to be cheerful.

As a rule, when you pick up a ukulele and give it a strum, the sound that emerges is pretty perky. It seems to call out, 'Hey-ho! Hee-hee! Woo-hoo!' Now, this is a wonderful thing about the ukulele, its in-built cheeriness, but at the same time it can be something a person can do without. How are we to indulge our melancholy feelings if we are surrounded by the jolly plucking of re-entrant strings? At times like these, it's wise to take a break from the ukulele, put on a miserable old album and wallow in your weariness. What a relief it will be to return to your little uke once you've shed a few good tears.

GOOD LUCK

Now that you've made it this far, there's not much left for me to say, apart from good luck. You now have all you need to go out and become an even better ukulele player, so it's time to do it your own way. Explore, have fun and be creative.

WORLDWIDE UKULELE WEB

A good way to find more ukulele goodies is by exploring the internet. It's fair to say that, without it, such a broad revival of the instrument might never have happened. Type 'ukulele' into your browser these days and literally millions of sites will appear, leading you ever deeper into the cyber world of the ukulele. For sympathizers, the internet offers the opportunity to talk about ukuleles without fear of ridicule, to meet other players and find out about their instruments, to swap music and (with the dawn of YouTube) watch countless ukulele video clips. YouTube has completely revolutionized people's access to musical history by bringing old footage from the 20th century directly into the 21st century at the click of a button. The budding enthusiast can now watch Cliff Edwards (aka 'Ukulele Ike' - see pages 20-1), Tiny Tim (see pages 22-3) and Tessie O'Shea (see page 31), and even listen to May Singhi Breen (see page 33) or Laura Dukes (see page 34), from the comfort of their own armchair.

Over the page are some ideas to whet your appetite. The ukulele world is your oyster.

REFERENCE

FIND OUT MORE

To fully appreciate the greatness of all the ukulele artists mentioned in this book, I thoroughly recommend that you visit YouTube, as simply reading about them can never do them justice. There is a smorgasbord of delights awaiting you on the web. In addition to all the legends listed in the Archdukes of Uke section (see pages 18-39), here are some other players you should check out while you're there...

☞ Roy Smeck - 'The Wizard of the Strings'; marvel at his use of the ukulele as a drum kit and whistle.

☞ Johnny Marvin - wonderful ukulele player and cheerful crooner of the 1920s.

☞ Herb Ohta - Hawaiian solo ukulele player performing beautiful jazz and pop standards.

☞ Lyle Ritz - American master of jazz uke with a talent for arranging tunes in chord form.

☞ Ukulelezaza - Terrific modern Dutch player and inventive ukulele tab arranger.

☞ Ernest Ka'ai - renowned Hawaiian ukulele maker, performer and author.

☞ John King - classical player and world authority on the ukulele.

☞ Sid Laverents - engineer, filmmaker and creator of the avant-garde classic film *Multiple SIDosis*, featuring a nice bit of uke.

☞ Max and Harry Nesbitt - classic vaudeville ukulele entertainers.

☞ Kuricorder Quartet - miniature music from Japan.

☞ Nigel Burch and the Flea-Pit Orchestra - my favourite cockney-Brechtian folk-punk banjo-ukulele band. Burch has been a champion of the uke since the early 1980s.

☞ Ukulele Uff & Lonesome Dave - Perfectly infectious Liverpudlian uke and guitar duo.

☞ The Hot Potato Syncopators - the hottest syncopators of potatoes in the UK.

☞ Petty Booka - Japanese duo playing Hawaiian, country and rock classics.

☞ Ian Emmerson and Phil Doleman - once formed the duo The Re-entrants. Do check out Ian's miniature ukulele solo on YouTube.

☞ Ewan Wardrop - Formby meets 50 Cent.

☞ Ukulele Club de Paris - Paris's very own Hot Club de Ukulele was founded in the 1980s.

☞ Sarah Maisel - Wonderful jazz ukuleleist from Alabama, USA.

☞ Aaron Keim - dustbowl ukulele Americana and a great online ukulele teacher.

☞ All Ukulele Orchestra of Great Britain members have great ukulele-shaped side projects that are worth exploring.

☞ Andy Eastwood - Self-confessed banjo-ukulele nut from Lancashire.

☞ Gus & Fin (GUGUG) - Knockout Scottish ukulele punk rockers.

UKULELE MUSIC TO LISTEN TO

☞ Cliff Edwards 'Ukulele Ike' - I recommend any compilation featuring 'My Red Hot Girl' or 'Paddlin' Madelin''.

☞ Tiny Tim - both *Tiny Tim (Live! At the Albert Hall)* and his first album, *God Bless Tiny Tim*, are well worth a listen.

☞ George Formby - his classics are 'Leaning on a Lampost' and 'The Window Cleaner' but look out for my favourite, 'Fanlight Fanny'.

☞ Ukulele Orchestra of Great Britain - there's lots to hear. Start off with the *Live...* album series, and check out the *Live at the Royal Albert Hall* and *Live at Sydney Opera House* DVDs.

☞ James Hill - *True Love Don't Weep*.

☞ Rabbit Muse - *Muse Blues* or *Sixty Minute Man* if you can track down these rare LPs.

☞ Roy Smeck - *Hawaiian Guitar, Banjo, Ukulele & Guitar* 1926-1949.

☞ George Harrison - *Brainwashed* includes a beautiful ukulele track 'Between the Devil and the Deep Blue Sea'.

☞ The Magnetic Fields - *69 Love Songs*.

☞ Lemon Nash - *Papa Lemon*.

☞ Mara Carlyle - *The Lovely* (especially 'Baby Bloodheart') and *Floreat*.

☞ Jake Shimabukuro - *Gently Weeps*.

☞ Charlie Burse & His Memphis Mudcats - *Memphis Shakedown*.

☞ Israel Kamakawiwo'ole - *Facing Future*.

☞ Laura Dukes - *Tennessee Blues No.1* features a few classic tracks.

☞ tUnE-yArDs - *Bird Brains* and *Whokill*.

☞ George Benson - *Inspiration: A Tribute to Nat King Cole* includes 'lil Georgie Benson playing 'Mona Lisa' on his uke.

☞ Nigel Burch and the Flea-Pit Orchestra - *Bottle Sucker*.

NOW WHAT? UKULELE PLACES

These days, ukulele jams and strum-alongs are taking place everywhere, from Mexico City to Dagenham, so there are all sorts of opportunities to get involved. Check out the internet for local ukulele clubs - this webpage is a great place to start: www.ukulelehunt. com/2010/03/10/ukulele-clubs-and-groups/

Joining a ukulele club is a good way to meet new people and to get strumming together. Ukulele festivals (and shops, too) are ubiquitous and spreading like wildfire. But perhaps the easiest way to get plugged into the ukulele scene is via the internet:

☞ www.ukulelehunt.com
   All-round tip-top ukulele resource

☞ www.ukulelecosmos.com
   Indispensable ukulele bantering

☞ www.ukuleleunderground.com
   Lessons, chat and more

☞ www.learntouke.co.uk
   Great UK-based ukulele teachers

☞ www.philsukelessons.blogspot.co.uk
   Uke tips and tricks from Phil

☞ www.nalu-music.com
   Ukulele information and history

☞ www.ukulele.fr
   Wonderful French ukulele site

☞ www.ukulele.nl
   Ace Dutch ukulele resource

☞ www.museuapa.com
   Add your machete to their collection

☞ www.chordmaster.org
   Plastic ukuleles a-go-go

☞ www.willgrovewhite.com
   More about the uke from me

☞ www.gotaukulele.com
   A hive of ukulele activity.

INDEX

SOURCES AND CREDITS

BOOKS

- Beloff, Jim, *The Ukulele: A Visual History*, Backbeat Books, 1997
- Bowman, David, *fa fa fa fa fa fa: The Adventures of Talking Heads in the 20th Century*, Bloomsbury, 2002
- Bret, David, *George Formby: A Troubled Genius*, Robson Books, 2001
- Byrne, David, *How Music Works*, Canongate, 2012
- Christie, Agatha, *Detectives and Young Adventurers: The Complete Short Stories*, HarperCollins, 2008
- Crowe, Julia, *My First Guitar: Tales of True Love and Lost Chords from 70 Legendary Musicians*, ECW Press, 2012
- Durchholz, Daniel and Graff, Gary, *Neil Young: Long May You Run*, Voyageur Press, 2010
- Dylan, Bob, *Chronicles*, Pocket Books, 2005
- Hendrix, Leon, *Jimi Hendrix: A Brother's Story*, St Martin's Griffin, 2013
- Hodgkinson, Tom and Pretor-Pinney, Gavin, *The Ukulele Handbook*, Bloomsbury, 2013
- McKee, Margaret and Chisenhall, Fred, *Beale Black & Blue: Life and Music on Black America's Main Street*, Louisiana State University Press, 1993
- Olsson, Bengt, *Memphis Blues and Jug Bands*, Studio Vista, 1970
- Salewicz, Chris, *Redemption Song: The Ballad of Joe Strummer*, Faber and Faber, 2007
- Tillery, Gary, *Working Class Mystic: A Spiritual Biography of George Harrison*, Quest Books, 2011
- Tranquada, Jim and King, John, *The Ukulele: A History*, University of Hawaii Press, 2012
- Trynka, Paul, *Starman: David Bowie*, Sphere, 2012
- Whitcomb, Ian, *Ukulele Heroes: The Golden Age*, Hal Leonard Corporation, 2012
- Wood, Alistair, *Ukulele for Dummies*, John Wiley & Sons, 2011
- Zimmer, David, ed. *Four Way Street: The Crosby, Stills, Nash & Young Reader*, Da Capo Press, 2004

ARTICLES

- Brodeur, Nicole, 'Eddie Vedder's "immediate gratification": a Martin ukulele', *The Seattle Times*, 2011
- 'Liverpool lads who played their way into our hearts', *Daily Express*, 5 September 2000
- Nagle, Patrick, '...Ssshhhhhh...Listen, Listen to Joni', *Weekend Magazine*, 1969
- Short, Don, 'Miss Vicki: My insufferable marriage to Tiny Tim', *Daily Mirror*, 22 December 1974
- Springer, Robert, 'I never did like to imitate nobody', *Blues Unlimited*, 1976
- 'The Prince's tour: visit to Port Elizabeth', *The Times*, 14 May 1925
- Udovitch, Mim and Wild, David, 'Remembering George', *Rolling Stone* #887, 2002
- 'Ukulele Slayer abandons fight for freedom', *San Jose News*, 12 February 1929
- Varga, George, 'Eddie Vedder on music, life and ukuleles', *U-T San Diego*, 2011
- Wilson, Dave, 'An interview with Joni Mitchell', *Broadside*, 1968

WEBSITES

www.chordmaster.org
www.elviscollectors.com
www.georgeformby.co.uk
www.gettyimages.co.uk
www.iwm.org.uk
www.jonimitchell.com
www.nalu-music.com
www.thepettyarchives.com
www.ukulele.fr
www.ukulelehunt.com
www.ullagegroup.com
www.wirz.de

PICTURE CREDITS

Alamy EPA European Pressphoto Agency b.v.: 78.
Don Blair: 66 right. Camera Press: Terence Spencer:
68. Antoine Carolus/UkeHeidi (www.chordmaster.
org): 53 left, 53 right, 55, 96. Jodi Cartwright: 11. Corbis:
Chuck Pulin/Splash News 73; John Springer Collection
20, 81; Romeo Ranoco/X00226/Reuters 94. Courtesy
of Autry Qualified Interest Trust: 14. Courtesy of Ian
Whitcomb: 38. Courtesy of Richard Nevins, Shanachie
Entertainment: (www.shanachie.com) 21. Courtesy of
University of Southern California, on behalf of the
USC Libraries Special Collections: 80. Andrew Downs/
BBC: 30. From the collection of António Rodrigues
(www.museuapa.com): 159. From the collection of Eliane
Maccaferri: 52. From the collection of Lyndon B Smith:
64. Getty Images: 82, 102; Bloomberg via Getty Images
66 left; Bruce Fleming 70; CBS via Getty Images 31; De
Agostini 42 right; Fiona Adams/Redferns 79; Hawaiian
Legacy Archive 49; IWM via Getty Images 25; Jessie
Tarbox Beals/The New York Historical Society 83;
John Kobal Foundation 48; Kevin Mazur/WireImage
57 above; Michael Ochs Archives 22, 72, 74, 75; Michael
Putland 69; Peter Still/Redferns 57 below; Roger
Kisby 158; Stephen J. Cohen 35; Thurston Hopkins 27;
UIG via Getty Images 42 left. Filipe Gomes, from the
collection of Norberto Gomes (www.museuapa.com):
1. Bob Gruen: 76. Hawaii State Archives: M-408, W R
Farrington's *Iolani Days Volume 2* Album 45; Photograph
Collection, PP-19-8-018 46; Photograph Collection,
PP-32-9a-023 47. James Hill (www.jameshillmusic.com):
Kevin Kelly: 36. Virginia Ironside: 7. Nichola Koratjitis:
169. Lebrecht Music & Arts Photofest: 33. George
Mitchell: 34 below. Mountain Apple Company HAWAII
(izhawaii.com): 32. NASA: 67. Photoshot Collection
Christophel: 63. Ron L. Saul: 165. Kirill Semkow (www.
semkow.de): 28. Blaine Shively: 39. Ukulele Afternoon:
37. Ukuleles for Peace (www.ukulelesforpeace.com): 59.

THANKS TO...

The Ukulele Orchestra of Great Britain (George
Hinchliffe, Kitty Lux, Jodi Cartwright, Dave Suich,
Peter Brooke Turner, Hester Goodman, Richie
Williams, Jonty Bankes, Ian Wood, Leisa Rea, Viola
Streich and Doug Beveridge), Ian Whitcomb, George
Benson and Stephanie Gonzalez, Pete Townshend
and Nicola Joss, Robert Crumb and Lora Fountain,
David Collard, Paul Willetts, Clare Alexander,
Lyndon B Smith, Victoria Taylor and Andrew Downs
(BBC Proms), Colin Fries and Jennifer Ross-Nazzal
at NASA, Ron and Thomas Boardman, Pete Howlett
(who made my ukulele - www.petehowlettukulele.
co.uk), Tony Bramwell, Philip Norman, Blaine Shively,
Bill Jefferson (www.wytiradio.com), John Hirasaki,
Don Blair, Keith Altham, George Underwood
(www.georgeunderwood.com), Ron L Saul, Eliane
Maccaferri, Paul Kessel, Stephan Wirz (www.wirz.de),
Antoine Carolus/UkeHeidi (www.chordmaster.org),
Jim and Liz Beloff (www.fleamarketmusic.com),
Kirill Semkow (www.semkow.de), Audrey Kimura,
Norberto Gomes, António Rodrigues and Filipe
Gomes (keen to add to their collection of Madeiran
machetes - www.museuapa.com), Richard Nevins
(www.shanachie.com), Phil Powell, Rufus Yells,
Scott Perry (www.scottperrymusician.com), Tom
Hodgkinson, Takatoshi Odajima and Ukulele
Afternoon (www.ukuleleafternoon.com), Julie Vandard
(www.uogbfrogsfan.org), Robin Gosden, James Hill,
Chalmers and Jean Doane, Virginia Ironside, Jonny
Hannah, Denis Whyte, Nichola Koratjitis, Otis and
Sid, Joe Brown and John Taylor, Paul Moore and
Daphna Orion (www.ukulelesforpeace.com). Finally,
thanks to Hannah Knowles, Leanne Bryan, Jen Veall,
Denise Bates, Jaz Bahra and Mr Jonathan Christie
at Octopus. Sorry if I've forgotten anyone. If I have,
I owe you a drink.

Will Grove-White is a musician, composer and writer,
and has been a member of the Ukulele Orchestra of
Great Britain since 1989. When not playing his ukulele,
he collects tiny things and makes tunes and noises for
TV and radio. He lives in South London. For more
information visit www.willgrovewhite.com

An indispensable bit of kit for any ukulele player's instrument case is a ukulele chord dictionary. This one shows pretty much every chord you're ever likely to need on one piece of paper, with suggested fingerings. Some of the more obscure chords may require yogic finger positioning, so if you find any too tricky, just play the notes you can manage, and don't play the ones you can't.

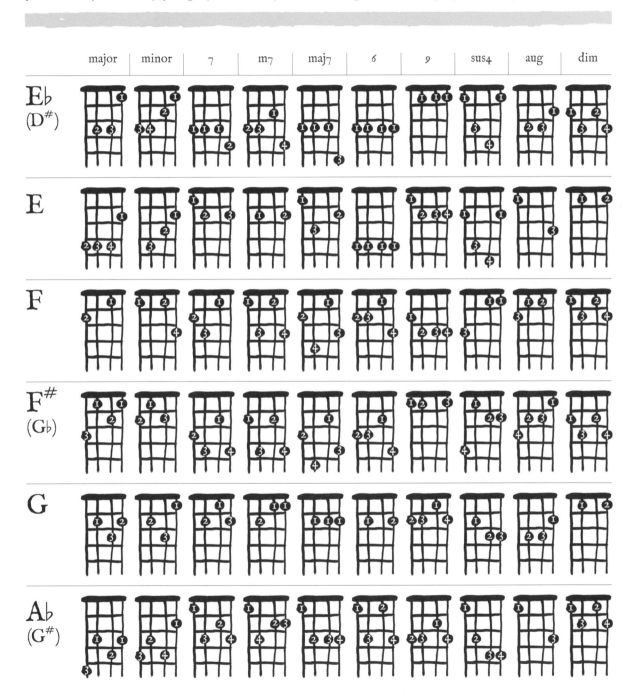

UKULELE CHORD DICTIONARY

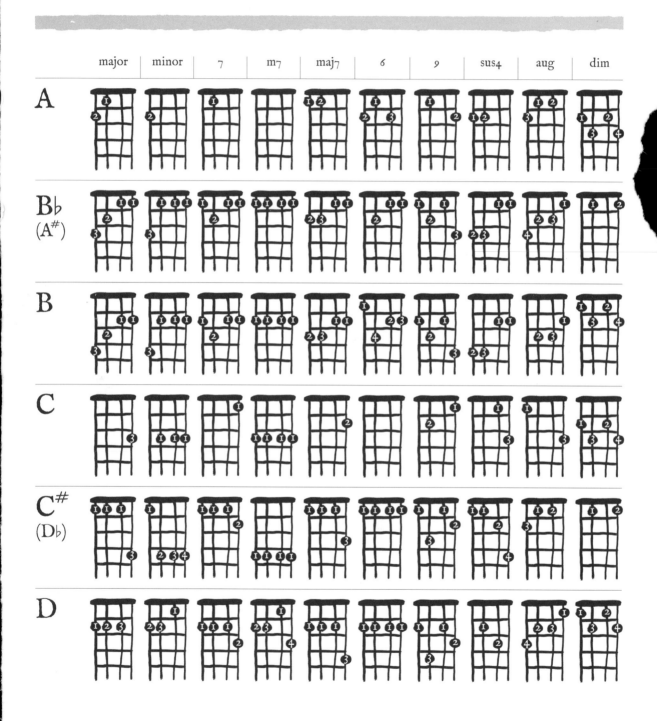